KV-241-612

INSTITUTE OF LEADERSHIP & MANAGEMENT ilm
SUPERSERIES

Marketing and Selling

FOURTH EDITION

Pergamon
Flexible
Learning

Published for the
Institute of Leadership & Management by

OXFORD   AMSTERDAM   BOSTON   LONDON   NEW YORK   PARIS
SAN DIEGO   SAN FRANCISCO   SINGAPORE   SYDNEY   TOKYO

Pergamon Flexible Learning
An imprint of Elsevier Science
Linacre House, Jordan Hill, Oxford OX2 8DP
200 Wheeler Road, Burlington, MA 01803

First published 1986
Second edition 1991
Third edition 1997
Fourth edition 2003

British Library Cataloguing in Publication Data
A catalogue record for this book is available from the British Library

ISBN 0 7506 58371

For information on Pergamon Flexible Learning
visit our website at www.bh.com/pergamonfl

Institute of Leadership & Management
registered office
1 Giltspur Street
London
EC1A 9DD
Telephone 020 7294 3053
www.i-l-m.com
ILM is a subsidiary of the City & Guilds Group

The views expressed in this work are those of the authors and do
not necessarily reflect those of the Institute of Leadership &
Management or of the publisher

Authors: Howard Senter and Jane Edmonds
Editor: Jane Edmonds
Editorial management: Genesys, www.genesys-consultants.com
Based on previous material by: Howard Senter
Composition by Genesis Typesetting, Rochester, Kent
Printed and bound in Great Britain by MPG Books, Bodmin

Contents

Contents

Workbook introduction

1 ILM Super Series study links

This workbook addresses the issues of *Marketing and Selling*. Should you wish to extend your study to other Super Series workbooks covering related or different subject areas, you will find a comprehensive list at the back of this book.

2 Links to ILM qualifications

This workbook relates to the following learning outcomes in segments from the ILM Level 3 Introductory Certificate in First Line Management and the Level 3 Certificate in First Line Management.

C3.8 Marketing
1 Understand the marketing concept and its relevance for managers
2 Understand the organization's key markets, customers and competition
3 Appreciate the organization's major marketing activities.

3 Links to S/NVQs in Management

This workbook relates to the following elements of the Management Standards which are used in S/NVQs in Management, as well as a range of other S/NVQs.

A1.3   Make recommendations for improvements to work activities
D1.1   Gather required information

It will also help you to develop the following Personal Competences:

- influencing others;
- focusing on results;
- searching for information.

4 Workbook objectives

'Marketing' has a kind of glamour. It makes us think of fashionable advertising agencies, and their high-flying 'creative teams', of costly and clever TV advertisements and large expense accounts.

Actually, this aspect of marketing is only the tip of the iceberg, and it is an area for specialists. Most managers, supervisors and team leaders will not take that route – they will work in the 'nuts and bolts' activities that keep the organization going from day to day.

There is another reason for steering away from the specialized aspects of marketing.

Slack & Mallarky Transport was a family firm. When the old boss's university-trained son took over the reins, he borrowed heavily and spent £380,000 on 'relaunching the business in the market place'.

There were new livery for the vehicles, uniforms for the drivers, new notepaper, an upgrade to the office and a trade advertising campaign. A sales manager was appointed at £46,000 a year plus car.

Soon after, the firm went into severe financial crisis and was bought out cheaply by a competitor.

The money spent on marketing did have an effect – sales initially increased but later fell back below what they had been before. Unfortunately, the new image was only skin-deep. The vehicles were smarter, but the service wasn't any more efficient. The office was full of new furniture, but information wasn't getting to customers any quicker. Worse, the cost of the 'marketing re-launch' was such that prices had to rise to cover it, leading to a loss of competitiveness that the new image was unable to redress.

The point is not that marketing campaigns are useless, but that there are limits on what they can achieve. Spending huge sums on advertising and publicity is no substitute for having the right product and an effective organization.

Success in the market depends primarily on offering customers a deal that is right – meaning as rapid, reliable, attractive, helpful and appropriate as possible for the price the customer is prepared to pay. And, in particular, it depends on being able to provide at least as good a deal as your competitors do.

The product or service on offer is only part of the deal. In the long run, the back-up, service, style and behaviour of every part of the organization has an impact on how far it meets the needs of its customers.

This is the marketing approach: making sure that everyone and everything in the organization is geared to meeting the needs of the market.

The implications should be clear. Every individual, every workteam, every manager, supervisor and team leader, whatever their specific function, does contribute in some way to market success or failure. You therefore have a responsibility to identify what you can do to support the marketing effort, and to lead your team in the right direction.

This workbook covers in some detail what it means to operate inside the market, what is meant by the marketing approach and what marketing actually consists of. The workbook also focuses on the many ways in which first line managers' work can help or hinder their organizations' marketing efforts.

4.1 Objectives

When you have completed this workbook, you will be better able to:

■ understand the meaning and importance of the market and the marketing approach;
■ describe the main activities and tools of marketing;
■ adopt the marketing approach and apply it to your everyday activities.

5 Activity planner

The following Activities require some planning so you may want to look at these now.

Activity 6 invites you to talk to other people in your organization to find a definition of the terms 'marketing' and the 'marketing approach'.

Activity 23 invites you to analyse your organization's range of products.

Activity 39 asks you to review what was done by your organization in terms of promotional and selling activity to market a new or recent product.

Activity 41 asks you to analyse the sales function in your organization.

Some or all of these Activities may provide the basis of evidence for your S/NVQ portfolio. All Portfolio Activities and the Work-based assignment are signposted with this icon.

The icon states the elements to which the Portfolio Activities and Work-based assignment relate.

The Work-based assignment involves reviewing what you and your team can do to provide your organization's customers with the right product, at the right price, the right place and at the right time. You may find it helpful to be thinking about these issues as you work through the sessions that follow.

Session A
Understanding the market

1 Introduction

Over the last 100 years whole industries have been swept away, and entirely new ones have come from nowhere. Caring for horses used to be one of the biggest service industries, with numerous stables in every town. Horse breeding was a large industry. On the light industrial side, tens of thousands of people earned their living by making harnesses and other equipment for horse-drawn vehicles. At the heavy end of the manufacturing spectrum, shipbuilding firms were thriving at ports everywhere in Britain. These were once major industries; today they have almost vanished.

On the other hand, even in the early 1970s there was virtually no computer industry, no satellite communications and no video business.

Why have the old industries disappeared? They could draw on tremendous skills and expertise, and they had dedicated workers. The products they produced were often first-rate. The problem was simply that their customers didn't want those products anymore – there were other products on offer that they preferred.

This is a most important lesson. People are justifiably proud of their skills and expertise, even of the equipment they use. They tend to focus on the product and forget the customer. But making a top-quality stage coach when the customer wants an economical two-ton van is the road to ruin.

This workbook is about changing focus, about thinking about the market and the customer first and the product itself second. This may sound topsy-turvy, but meeting the customers' needs is what counts, and the product itself is just one part of that. As you will see, this focus on customers' needs is, in fact, what the concept of marketing is all about.

2 The market and competition

The word 'market' is used in many different contexts, for example:

- the Stock Market;
- the cattle market;
- the European Single Market;
- the export market;
- the money market;
- the commodities market.

2.1 What is the 'market'?

What do all these markets have in common?

Activity 1 ·   8 mins

Think about your local open market – perhaps a fruit and vegetable market. Describe in about fifty words what goes on there.

_____

_____

_____

_____

_____

_____

_____

_____

I would describe it as follows:

> A number of different traders bring their goods and set them out on stalls. Then lots of potential customers come along and decide what they will buy, and from which trader they will buy it. The traders each try to sell their goods by offering the customer sharper pricing, or more attractive displays, or by shouting louder.

There are two things to notice about this description.

- The market forces the trader to face competition.
- The market presents the customer with choice.

However, the term 'market' in a general sense refers to a whole economic system which is conducted on this basis.

The market is simply the way in which the supply of goods and services, both nationally and internationally, is organized – though 'organized' is perhaps the wrong word to use about it. The market is not organized in the way that a factory or an office is. It is the net product of limitless numbers of buyers meeting limitless numbers of sellers, which results in millions of individual purchasing decisions. The market is constantly changing and therefore very difficult to predict. It is almost impossible to control, except in very limited and specialized areas where there are few sellers and buyers.

But the market determines whether or not a particular product will succeed. This is the so-called 'law of supply and demand', and in this respect, the market is a mechanism for deciding, on a global scale, what goods and services will be produced and how much they can be sold for.

Every organization operates inside the market and, in some sense, lays its wares out on a stall in front of the buying public. For commercial organizations, success in the market is obviously crucial because it brings in the profits needed for survival. However, the 'market approach' has become relevant to non-commercial organizations too – from hospitals, schools and government departments right down to voluntary bodies, social services departments and even prisons.

They all need to market themselves: they need funds, equipment, staff, 'clients', volunteer workers, donations and so on. And, just like industry and commerce, they have to compete to get them.

2.2 The product

People who work in the manufacturing industry will naturally think of the things they make as 'products'. These may be pipes or pickles, tanks or tintacks, but they are something physical that they can point to and say: 'That's our product.'

However, from the marketing standpoint, the term 'product' includes both physical objects of various kinds and what is usually thought of as services, such as insurance policies or TV rental packages.

Activity 2
3 mins

List **five** 'products' offered by a typical high-street bank or building society.

_____

_____

_____

_____

_____

Financial institutions have many products (they do actually refer to them as 'products'). They include current accounts, deposit accounts, ISAs, mortgages, loans, foreign exchange, bill payment services, insurance, savings plans, pensions schemes and so on.

These are what the banks or building societies try to 'sell' in their part of the market.

> When a supermarket sells a piece of steak, what is the customer really buying? Not nourishment as such, because that could come from lentils, bread or tinned salmon. What the customer is really buying is a highly satisfying idea – the sizzle, not the steak, as marketing people often put it.

Throughout this workbook the word 'product' refers to whatever an organization has to offer to the market, whether that is goods, services or something else.

Something else? Some business experts believe that there is really only ever one product – satisfaction. That's over-simplifying things, but whatever kind of organization you work for, you should always remember that there is no future unless you can satisfy your customers' needs or desires.

2.3 Monopoly and competition

Imagine a world where there was only one source of a particular important product – say smoke detectors. This situation is known as a monopoly.

Everyone who wanted a smoke detector badly enough would have to go to that one supplier. The supplier wouldn't need to try very hard.

■ There would be no need to bother with appearances: the business could be run from a dirty old shed.
■ Convenience wouldn't matter much either: the firm could be located in Greenland.
■ Publicity and promotion could be ignored – the customers would tell each other where to find the supplier.
■ Service, packaging, quality and price would be of no importance.

In practice, monopolies are rather rare. In every area of activity that is capable of being profitable, there is always competition.

Activity 3

10 mins

Here are three different enterprises. For each one, say who its competitors might be and why.

The Tower of London

_____

_____

_____

Your local travel agent

_____

_____

_____

Tesco

_____

_____

_____

'The customer rarely buys what the business thinks it sells him. One reason for this, of course, is that nobody pays for a 'product'. What is paid for is satisfactions ... Because the customer buys satisfactions, all goods and services compete intensively with goods and services that look quite different, seem to serve entirely different functions, are made, distributed, sold differently – but are alternative means for the customer to obtain satisfaction.'

Peter Drucker,
Managing for Results

The easiest of these to answer is the third one. Tesco competes for customers with other supermarkets both in Britain and in various other countries in Europe and Asia.

The first example, a famous tourist attraction, may have given you pause for thought. But tourist attractions do have to compete, even if many visitors specifically want to visit this particular place. In the long run, if the Tower of London were to become too expensive, or too shoddy, or if the staff were too unhelpful, it would lose out to other tourist attractions. So the Tower of London is in competition with all the other tourist sites in London.

To some extent the Tower also competes with other cities – Cambridge, Edinburgh, Paris or Rome – because it is part of London's general 'competitive pitch' for the international tourist market. And you can go a step further: the Tower also competes with other things that people could be spending their time and money doing, from watching TV to taking a river trip or going to the races.

The same applies to the local travel agent. Each travel agent has to compete with its business rivals, but it also has to compete with other products that families might spend their money on. A sum of £700 spent on a holiday could have been spent on new carpets, a hi-fi or dozens of other things.

So there are two points here.

- Every organized enterprise faces competition.
- Competition does not necessarily come just from the obvious business rivals.

Activity 4 · 5 mins

Now think about your own organization (or one that you know well).

a What are its main products?

_____

_____

_____

b Who are its main competitors?

_____

_____

_____

In thinking about these questions you have probably found that your organization does have competitors. You will see that, whatever part of the organization you work in, how you deal with that competition is a key issue for every employee in your organization.

Successful competition demands hard work, clear vision, skills and resources.

- The penalties of failure are decline, job losses, and eventually bankruptcy or take-over.
- The rewards of success are growth, expansion and opportunity.

3 Product life-cycles

You saw in the last section that the 'market' is all about the buying and selling of products – goods, services or whatever. But the market has a ruthless way with products, and even the most successful product has a limited life-cycle. The market is constantly changing, and unless the products also change, they will be left behind and forgotten.

Organizations that want to survive longer than any of the particular products they offer, must do two things.

- They must modify existing products to ensure that they meet the requirements of today's market.
- They must introduce new products that will meet the needs of tomorrow's market.

In the business world this has produced some remarkable changes. One of the most spectacular transformations was that of the firm that makes Rose's Lime Juice. In the nineteenth century, it was a shipping company, and it supplied its sailors with lime juice to prevent scurvy. As the markets changed, the firm abandoned the shipping operation and concentrated on the lime-juice business!

Everyone knows the story of how, in the nineteenth century, lime juice was introduced to prevent scurvy. This unpleasant disease, which was once almost universal among sailors who went on long voyages, was purely the result of poor diet. What most people don't know is that lemon juice is actually far more effective at preventing scurvy, but that the British Navy switched to limes because they were cheaper – a market decision!

Activity 5 · 3 mins

What new products (or services) has the organization you work for introduced in the last three years?

_____

_____

_____

It would be unusual if there weren't any new products – and it would be a danger sign. New products need to be developed to replace those that will soon go into decline. However, it may have occurred to you that another approach to this problem is to revamp existing products in various ways. The big car manufacturers are a good example of this. The Ford Fiesta, the Vauxhall Astra and the Peugeot 306 have been around for many years, but every two or three years the manufacturers carry out a significant upgrade and relaunch improved models on the market.

Successful commercial products typically pass through a four-stage life-cycle.

■ Stage 1

Research, development, tooling and planning, production, promotion, advertising and launch on the market.

■ Stage 2

Rapid sales growth, competitive advantage and high profits.

■ Stage 3

Sales still good, but competition increasing and profitability declining (the market is 'mature'). This is the stage where upgrades are typically made, to try to prolong the product's useful life as a profit-maker.

■ Stage 4

Product outdated, fierce competition, price falling, sales and profits in decline (the market is 'saturated').

Of course, some products live longer than others, while many never get beyond stage 2.

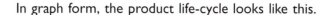

In graph form, the product life-cycle looks like this.

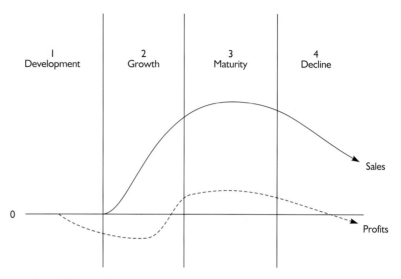

The product life cycle

Clearly, before the sales line starts dropping in stage 3, new products must come into the picture, so that sales are kept stable overall.

The 80:20 rule (Pareto's Law) applies to products sold in the market: 80 per cent of the profit comes from 20 per cent of the products.

Because predicting the way the market will move in future is so difficult, most new products do not do well. The proportion that succeed in a big way is tiny (perhaps only 1%) and most businesses try to keep up a steady flow of product innovation so that the chances of at least one product succeeding are reasonably high.

But even though it is difficult, the better we can predict the market, the less the risk of failure. That is an essential part of the marketing approach.

4 The marketing approach

For most people, the word 'marketing' conjures up the 'sharp end' activities such as planning advertising campaigns and getting the sales team mobilized.

4.1 A definition

This is indeed one part of marketing, but there is much more to it.

Activity 6 · 20 mins

S/NVQ D1.1

This Activity may provide the basis of appropriate evidence for your S/NVQ portfolio. If you are intending to take this course of action, it might be better to write your answers on separate sheets of paper.

Talk to the people in your organization who are responsible for marketing, or its equivalent. Ask them how they would define 'marketing', then summarize your findings here.

_____

_____

_____

Also ask them what they understand by 'the marketing approach', and summarize that similarly.

_____

_____

_____

Finally, consider what this implies for you and your workteam. Note down any points that hadn't occurred to you before.

_____

_____

_____

_____

There are several accepted definitions of marketing. A narrow one might be:

Marketing is about promoting the product to the customer.

However, promotion is only one small part of marketing. Nowadays, most organizations define marketing along the following lines.

Marketing is about identifying and satisfying the needs of customers by providing the right product at the right price, time and place.

In other words, marketing is about identifying:

■ what product (whether it be in the form of goods or a service) the customer wants;
■ the price customers are prepared to pay for the product;
■ the place and time at which the product must be available.

Of course, customers need to know about the product, so marketing is also about promotion.

You may have noticed that four words beginning with 'P' feature in the definition above. These are referred to as the 'four Ps':

■ product;
■ price;
■ place;
■ promotion.

Together the 'four Ps' form what is known as the 'marketing mix', a subject to which we will return in session B. Here we are going to focus on the marketing approach, which is all about identifying and meeting customer needs. In the case of private sector organizations, it is also about meeting these needs profitably. The following motto sums up this approach.

'Love the customer, not the product.'

You don't have to be in the marketing department to play a role in marketing your organization. Any manager who strives to ensure that their staff help to meet customer needs is playing a part in marketing their organization. But first they need to know what these needs are. This is where market research comes in.

4.2 Market research

Market research is about gaining greater knowledge and understanding of the market. It is a vitally important part of the marketing approach. But what knowledge do we need?

Activity 7

5 mins

Ted and Lucy came into some money, and decided to give up their jobs to start a business making and selling radio-controlled models.

What would you say were the **three** most important aspects of the market that they would need to research before making the decision to begin?

_____

_____

_____

EXTENSION 1
Market research is a way of getting reliable information about important issues. Any manager may find the basic skills useful from time to time. If you would like to go into the subject of market research in more depth and learn about some of the techniques involved, you might like to read _Do Your Own Market Research_ by P.N. Hague and P. Jackson.

It is most important to find out about the total size and money value of the market, and the nature and strength of the competition as they are at present.

- How many people in the area are interested in these products;
- How much they are likely to spend on them;
- Who the competitors are, what they do and where they are located.

Activity 8

3 mins

It is difficult for market research to predict the future, but try to suggest **three** things that researchers could investigate to help Ted and Lucy assess the future potential of the market for radio-controlled models.

_____

_____

_____

_____

This activity may have been difficult for you if you have no previous knowledge of marketing, but perhaps you gave some thought to the sort of people who might be (or become) interested in expensive toys such as radio-controlled cars.

■ What sort of people they are likely to be.
■ How many such people there are.
■ Whether their numbers are likely to increase or decrease.
■ What might be done to turn these potential customers into actual customers.

Market research is getting more sophisticated. Increasingly it is focusing on:

■ lifestyles and attitudes rather than simply income and spending patterns;
■ general economic changes that will influence spending patterns over a period of years.

The tasks of market research can be summed up as follows.

> **Market research needs to find out the present state of the market and how it is likely to change in the future.**

This applies to every kind of organization which operates in a market, whether its products are goods or services, whether it is large or small, and whether its market is local, national or international.

Market research is very big business – but it does not take decisions. That can be done only by managers, using the research figures, and perhaps helped by marketing specialists.

4.3 Market-led or product-led?

Every organization has to decide what attitude it will take towards its product and its customers.

Activity 9 · 3 mins

Which of these three attitudes is closest to that of your own organization?

Build a better mousetrap, and the world will beat a path to your door. ☐

Build a worse mousetrap, and spend a lot of money on advertising, and the world will beat a path to your door. ☐

Find out what sort of a mousetrap customers want, then produce it and tell them. ☐

The people who design and develop a new product are usually experts in their subject. Whether it is an insurance firm planning a new policy for people buying holiday homes abroad, or an electronics company designing a new type of car alarm, highly experienced and expert people will be involved.

However, left to themselves, the experts may come up with a product which does its job brilliantly but is too complex and expensive for the market. It may be 'over-engineered', in design terms. That is the 'build a better mousetrap' attitude: a **product-led** operation.

Product-led organizations can find themselves deeply disappointed when their superb product fails to sell because it was what **they** wanted, but not what the **customer** wanted.

On the other hand, those organizations which don't care about product quality at all but expect the marketing people to 'hype' their way to success are also doomed to failure: a worse mousetrap will soon be seen for what it is.

The third attitude is more likely to be successful. The needs of the market override the needs of the product and its designers, so **market-led** organizations:

- first study their market;
- then give the development and production people a specification designed to meet the market's needs;
- then get the product produced;
- then promote it in a positive and effective way.

Product distribution

The best promotional campaign can fail if the product isn't ready **and right** when it's needed. One of the worst disasters that can happen in marketing is for the customers to be ready and eager to take up a new product, only to find that some problem has held up delivery for days or even weeks.

A new range of six different easy-cook meals was due to hit the shops on 1 June. The advertising campaign was booked, with adverts on TV and in household and general interest magazines. Placards and special 'point of sale' materials were waiting at the retailers. A massive direct mail campaign was about to send millions of 'special offer' vouchers plopping onto consumers' doormats. 'Demonstrators' had been hired to promote the product in local stores.

Then, at the very last minute, disaster struck. The marketing people had assumed that a mixture of all six meals would be supplied to all the retail outlets, but no one had checked these arrangements with the production department. The factory had therefore gone for efficiency: it had made large runs of each individual meal and stored them in batches of 360 in special containers.

Someone was going to have to break all these up and repack them into mixed batches. The distribution company agreed to do this, but it was extremely expensive. It also took two days to complete. So, on 1 June, no products were available in the shops. Many retailers, unwilling to display empty promotional stands, cancelled their orders. Those that did persist, found that the shelf life of the meals was only three days instead of the expected five days. This caused all sorts of additional complications and ill-will.

In supermarkets you will certainly have seen special promotional displays (often at the ends of aisles where they get most exposure). What you may not realize is that the selling power of these sites is so great that retailers can often **charge** suppliers for the privilege of placing their products there.

If the distribution arrangements aren't right, even the most brilliant marketing campaign will be a waste of time and money.

Self-assessment 1

15 mins

1   Fill in the blanks so that these statements make sense.

a   The market forces traders to face _____ and presents customers with _____.

b   The market is the net result of millions of individual _____ _____.

c   The term _____ refers to whatever an organization offers to the market.

d   Even the most successful product has a limited _____ _____.

e   Market research is about gaining greater _____ and _____ of the market.

2   Which of the following best describes the marketing approach?

a   It is about selling an organization's products.
b   It is about identifying what the market is for an organizations' product.
c   It is about identifying and satisfying customer needs.
d   It is about establishing the right price for the product.

3   Fill in the blanks.

A _____ organization is one that studies its market before getting a product produced. A _____ organization is one that produces what it considers to be a superb product first and then sets about discovering whether it is what customers want.

Answers to these questions can be found on page 95.

5 Summary

- The market is a system under which large numbers of traders offer goods or services for sale and large numbers of customers choose which to buy. The market is the net product of millions of individual purchasing decisions.

- Almost every organized enterprise faces competition; monopolies are rare.

- Competition does not necessarily come from the obvious business rivals.

- The goods, services or activities that an organization markets are known in general as its 'products'.

- All products have a limited life-cycle. Commercial organizations need to keep developing new products, to ensure their long-term survival.

- Marketing can be defined as 'The process of identifying and satisfying the needs of customers by providing the right product at the right price, time and place.'

- What is referred to as the 'marketing mix' is made up of the 'four Ps':

  - product;
  - price;
  - place;
  - promotion.

- Every aspect of an organization is relevant to its success or failure in the market.

- Market research looks mainly at the existing market with regard to:

  - the number and location of the customers;
  - how much they have to spend;
  - who the competitors are.

- Market research also tries to predict how the market will be in the future; but this is difficult.

- 'Product-led' organizations start with their products, and then look for ways of marketing them.

- 'Market-led' organizations:

  - first study their market;
  - then specify a product that will meet the market's needs;
  - then produce the product;
  - then promote it effectively.

- The most successful organizations are market-led and adopt a 'total marketing approach'.

Session B
The marketing mix

1 Introduction

'The marketing mix' is a jargon term, but the idea behind it is very significant, because every product on the market is different, even if the differences only seem small.

Take petrol, for example. All petrol of the same grade is basically the same regardless of whether it is sold by Shell, Texaco, BP or anyone else. Even the price does not vary greatly between different petrol retailers in the same locality. However, every petrol company presents its petrol to the public in a slightly different way. Some have a mini supermarket on the forecourt, others just a small shop. Some offer tokens, gifts, loyalty cards and other promotional inducements, others don't. Some concentrate on big trunk-road sites, others go for smaller urban locations. Some put their staff in uniform, others don't. And overall, the style, decor, layout and advertising of the different companies are distinctly different.

All the details that distinguish a BP station from a Texaco station, and from all the others, play a part in building up the overall 'package' that the company offers to its customers. Individually, the impact of the details may be quite small, but together they make up a distinctive **marketing mix**. (And, actually, the petrol is the least important part of the marketing mix for petrol companies: their marketing people regard the petrol station as the product, not the fuel sold there.)

These differences are crucial in enabling the rivals to compete. They cannot truthfully say things like 'Buy Octopus petrol because it makes your car go faster', but they can say 'Buy Octopus petrol because our service is better', or 'because our stations are cleaner and more modern' or 'because we share your particular lifestyle'.

2 The elements of the marketing mix

The marketing mix is the sum total of all the things that an organization does that have some impact on customers' attitudes to its product – the total 'offer' that an organization makes to its market. Broadly, the elements are those we looked at briefly in Session A:

- product;
- price;
- place;
- promotion.

An organization that gets all these elements right may not sweep the market, but it will be able to compete; one that doesn't won't even be in the running. This applies to non-commercial organizations as well as those whose main objective is to make profits. So what does each of these elements consist of?

2.1 Defining the 'four Ps'

- **Product**
  A product, whether it is a physical item or service, is made up of a number of elements that can include:

  - its features;
  - its design;
  - its quality;
  - the way it's packaged;
  - an accompanying guarantee and/or statement of conditions for its return;
  - back-up services.

Take the example of a personal computer. The PC's features may include the amount of RAM memory, the size of the hard drive, the monitor, speakers, sound card, keyboard, mouse, floppy disk drive, zip drive, CD writer, DVD/CD drive, modem, one or more software packages, and so on. The design of the casing for the various components could be in tower form or flat, and in one or more of a range of colours. The quality will depend on how reliable the components are and how carefully they are assembled together. The computer may come with a one to three-year guarantee; with a promise of a free visit from an engineer within 24 hours of being called out and repairs on site – or a service that involves taking the computer away. There may be a helpline to connect the customer to a technical adviser. If so, how long is the average wait in the queuing system? Finally, the computer and the accompanying peripherals will arrive in packaging that hopefully will be good enough to have prevented anything being damaged during transit.

This is the total product. But in deciding whether to buy a particular PC, this will not be the only thing that the customer will take into account.

- **Price**
  The price will also have a major part to play in any customer's decision. A higher than average price will not necessarily deter a customer who wants to be sure that they are receiving a quality product. Deciding on what the balance should be between price and quality is a marketing decision that will partly be based on what type of customer the company is aiming for. The price is not just the listed price. It is also any discounts available for purchasing at a particular time or any credit terms that are available.

- **Place**
  Another factor that the customer will take into account is exactly where – and when – they can purchase the computer. Do they need to go to a retail outlet to purchase it – or can they just place an order over the phone or through the Internet? Either way, what are the hours during which they can make their purchase? Can they purchase in the evenings and on Sundays? If the computer is being sold through a retail outlet, how good are the transport facilities to the outlet? Is it easy to park a car nearby?

- **Promotion**
  The final major factor that will influence the customer in making their decision about what computer to buy is the way it is promoted. Is it advertised on the TV or radio – or through the Internet and regular mail-shots? Is telemarketing used? When the customer decides to ring the company (if business is all done over the phone) or visit the retail outlet, how are they treated by the salesforce? Are the salesforce well-informed and prepared to take their time giving the customer advice and making them feel valued – or do they make the customer feel as though no one cares whether they place an order or not?

All these factors contribute to the marketing mix that will influence the customer in making a decision about what and where to buy. They are summarized in the diagram below.

Typical elements in the marketing mix for a product

We have looked at the components of a marketing mix for a physical item – but all are equally relevant to a service, as the next activity will show.

Activity 10

5 mins

Imagine you are fed up with the service you are receiving from your bank and you decide to look at the other banks and building societies near your home to decide if it's worth moving your account to any of them. What kinds of factors will affect your choice under the following headings?

Product

_____

_____

_____

Price

_____

_____

_____

Place

_____

_____

_____

Promotion

_____

_____

_____

■ Product
A typical bank or building society offers a number of services, including:

- current accounts;
- deposit/savings accounts;
- credit cards;
- loans and mortgages;
- life and general insurance;
- pensions.

Each of these services has a number of features. With the credit card, for example, comes a particular rate of interest, an annual fee or no annual fee, a stipulated number of days of interest-free credit, a credit limit, and possibly a points system under which points are exchanged for vouchers or reductions in certain bills.

When it comes to quality, it is important to consider the bank or building society as a whole. Does it offer telephone or on-line banking services? What is the attitude of the staff – are they friendly and helpful? Do they seem to have enough knowledge and expertise to talk sensibly about your needs? Are enough of them on duty during busy periods so that you don't have to queue for long?

Other factors to consider are the general style and décor of the premises. Are they smart, clean, and kept at a comfortable temperature. Are notices, leaflets and forms neatly and clearly displayed? Is there a place where it's possible to sit down and discuss the services being offered with a member of staff?

■ Price

There are all sorts of factors related to price that might affect your choice, such as:

- ■ interest earned on current account;
- ■ interest earned on deposit or savings accounts;
- ■ account charges;
- ■ interest charges on loans and mortgages.

■ Place

You will want the bank or building society to be conveniently located – that is, in a place you can get to easily and perhaps close to car parking and other facilities, such as shops. The time at which it is open is also important. Will it be open when you need it?

■ Promotion

Finally, there is the image of the bank or building society created by its advertising. Many spend large sums on TV advertising to build a particular image, which may be caring, efficient, business-like, hi-tech, relaxed and friendly, and so on. Like the décor and window display of their local branches, these are not necessarily factors of which you are conscious when you make buying decisions, but they affect you subconsciously – perhaps more than the promotional material that banks and building societies generally have on display at their premises.

EXTENSION 2
If you would like to find out more about the elements of the marketing mix, try reading the relevant sections in *Marketing Made Simple* by G. Lancaster and P. Reynolds. This book contains many examples illustrating how an organization must pay full attention to all 'four Ps' if it is to ensure continuing success in the market.

In summary, the marketing mix has a number of important aspects:

- ■ everything that has an effect on the customer is part of it, and this is true whether those concerned are aware of it or not;
- ■ some factors weigh more heavily than others;
- ■ customers make conscious decisions about some factors, but others have a subconscious effect.

3 Product quality

As a manager, one of the ways in which you can contribute to the marketing of a product is in achieving quality. This is sometimes defined as providing a product or service that meets the needs of customers at prices they can afford. But achieving quality can also mean continually improving a product or service so that it meets these needs in the future and pleases customers to such an extent that they tell other people about it. It is worth remembering that research has shown that when a person is happy about an item they have purchased, they tell an average of four people about it. However, when they are unhappy about a purchase because, for example, it wears out or breaks down more quickly than expected, they tell an average of sixteen people about it.

Customers do not expect Rolls-Royce standards from a car at or near the bottom of the price range. But they do expect their car to conform to certain standards. Problems arise when the quality falls below what the customer expects for the price paid, and when the back-up services do not meet the customer's expectations.

3.1   Maintaining standards of quality

Lee & Sherrills, a leading food manufacturer, were able to buy ground almonds from a number of countries and via various different suppliers, with very little variation in price. As it happened, they normally bought them from Turkey, through a supplier with whom they had a good relationship. Then problems began to arise. One consignment had to be rejected because it was contaminated with chlorine. Next, the colour of the product changed from white to a pale beige. Finally, there were hold-ups when the supplier was unable to deliver on time.

L&S were reluctant to abandon their old-established supplier and pressed them for guarantees of quality and supply for the future, but these did not solve the problems. So they simply switched to another source, and the original supplier lost the account, even though they offered to drop the price.

Activity 11   2 mins

Contracts can easily be lost owing to production problems. What would you say were the supplier's **two** major shortcomings?

_____

_____

_____

_____

First, they did not monitor the production quality properly. Someone must have known that the quality was falling, but nothing was done about it. Second, they failed to meet the customer's delivery dates. It is easy for suppliers to become sloppy about this, but if the customer needs everything exactly at the right time in order to start a production run, then it is a major problem.

There was also a third problem – the supplier did not put things right when the customer complained.

Quality usually means reliability too. Lee & Sherrills' original supplier lost their contract because they became unreliable. Most commercial customers place a value on reliability and consistency and are prepared to pay more for it. This is another pointer to how managers, supervisors and team leaders in all areas of an organization can help the marketing effort.

4 Maintaining customer satisfaction

So far we have considered the marketing mix in terms of encouraging customers to purchase a product or service in the first place. However, an organization that concentrates on getting the initial 'offer' right, but then pays little attention to ensuring the long-term loyalty of its customers, will not survive in a competitive environment.

Activity 12 3 mins

Long-term customer loyalty may be vital for the survival of both the bank or building society and the computer manufacturer and retailer. List **three** factors which could influence customers to stay with, or to desert, their supplier:

_____

_____

_____

The most important factor is likely to be the **performance** of the product. If a piece of equipment continually breaks down or underperforms, the customer is likely to become very disillusioned with the supplier. If the deposit or savings account turns out to offer lower interest and less flexible terms than other products, including new ones entering the market, the bank's or building society's customer may close his or her account and switch to a competitor.

'Behind-the-scenes' factors also affect customer satisfaction, for example:

- the speed with which the supplier's staff tackle problems and queries;
- their attitude when doing so (which can vary from being eager to help to being downright hostile);
- the general efficiency of the organization (including details like spelling the customer's name right; sending post or deliveries to the right address; getting financial details correct first time; keeping a record of conversations, messages and appointments).

The importance of always being prepared to tackle customers' problems and queries is illustrated by the following example.

> Janet was office supervisor for a firm of architects. One Monday morning in January she found that the special machine used for outputting large-scale architectural drawings from the computer database was not working.
>
> The senior partner urgently needed to output three important drawings, which he had been altering over the weekend. Janet phoned their usual equipment maintenance people and tried to explain her problem. An uninterested voice interrupted her to say: 'Don't worry, it's the cold you know. It'll sort itself out. Give us a ring back at lunchtime if it doesn't and we'll see what we can do.'
>
> Janet then searched through the *Yellow Pages* and found another maintenance firm. An interested voice assured her that they would be able to help and then listened while she explained her problem.
>
> 'It's probably not a serious fault, just the cold weather. Some machines can be affected like that. Try to get some heat onto the machine – just gentle heat or you may do some damage. In the meantime I'll re-route one of our service engineers, so there should be someone there within the hour.'

Activity 13 · 3 mins

Write down a few of the words that you might use to describe the approach of the two firms that Janet tried.

The original firm:

_____

_____

The new firm:

_____

_____

I think most experts would make a judgement like this.

- The original firm: inefficient, couldn't-care-less, useless, disorganized, complacent, sloppy.
- The new firm: efficient, helpful, concerned, organized, keen – and willing to 'go the extra mile' to please a customer.

The original firm is likely to be on the way out; the newcomers may have won a new account.

4.1 Dealing with dissatisfaction

Problems and complaints have a crucial influence on the long-term marketing position of any organization. Naturally, it is a good idea to produce a quality product with a minimum of faults and errors, but no one is perfect, and problems will occur in the most excellent of products. It is what happens after the customer has reported the problem that counts. Here is an example.

> Sheena rented a TV and video from Rapid Rentals. As part of the deal, it offered a refund if a repair took longer than forty-eight hours.
>
> One day, the TV broke down, and Sheena reported it. The following day, an engineer arrived and fixed it.
>
> Three days later, it broke down again. The engineer came after two days and fixed it.

A week later, it broke down again. This time, the engineer did not come. After ten days, Sheena complained in writing to the managing director of Rapid Rentals, and asked for the equipment to be removed and a refund given for the time it hadn't been working.

She received a very polite and apologetic letter from the MD, and the firm was prompt to remove the equipment and issue the refund. A few days later, however, Sheena received a letter from Rapid Rentals' accounts department, demanding a rental payment for equipment she no longer had. She returned this with a further letter to the MD. This time, the customer services manager wrote back apologising for the mix-up.

That should have been the end of the matter – except that within days Sheena received from the accounts department a new paying-in book for the following year!

Activity 14

5 mins

What would you say went wrong in the case of Sheena and the rental firm?

_____

_____

_____

_____

Clearly, the firm was badly organized: the left hand didn't know what the right hand was doing, and this always leads to problems. But organizational problems are always someone's responsibility.

- **Someone** should have noticed that this TV had broken down three times in rapid succession and done something about it.
- **Someone** should have made sure that when the rental contract was cancelled, the accounts department were informed.

Perhaps this organization should have employed a team of people specifically to ensure that service quality matched the promises the firm gave its customers!

Activity 15

5 mins

No organization likes receiving complaints, but a number of leading companies now take the view that complaints can be positively beneficial in increasing customer loyalty. Try to suggest why this might be.

_____

_____

_____

_____

The logic goes like this.

> Bad news travels faster than good. Research has shown that when customers are satisfied, they tell around four other people. But when they are dissatisfied, they tell an average of sixteen.

- Some customers do not complain, they simply 'vote with their feet', i.e. they stop using the organization and go to a competitor next time.
- The long-term attitude of those who do complain depends on how well an organization deals with the complaint; customers whose problem is promptly, efficiently and pleasantly resolved are likely to have a **higher opinion** of the organization than they did before the problem arose; they become more loyal, not less.
- Complaints are an important source of feedback about how well a product is performing; if you listen carefully and take the necessary measures, you can improve your product in the future.

Activity 16

8 mins

If you are involved in the production of a product or delivery of a service – either directly or indirectly – think of two ways in which you, and any staff you supervise, might do more to maintain customer satisfaction and so reduce the number of complaints.

_____

_____

_____

_____

5 The people factor in the marketing mix

Every single aspect of an organization that a customer encounters will have some impact on that customer's attitude and therefore on his or her purchasing decisions.

Each aspect will either strengthen or weaken the organization's ability to succeed in the market. The effect of any one element in the marketing mix may be quite small, but even a very small 'minus point' may be enough to let in a competitor whose 'package' is marginally more attractive.

In this 'total' approach, it is obvious that people and the way they deal with customers will be particularly important. Every employee whose activities have an effect on the product or the customer contributes to market success or failure. In fact, the most successful organizations believe that **everyone on their payroll** is part of the marketing mix.

Activity 17

12 mins

Here are four short descriptions of people working in quite different kinds of jobs. Think about each situation carefully, and then write down what you think about the impact on the organizations' marketing mix.

Sarah was credit control supervisor with a large firm of builders' merchants. She and her team spent at least three days every month chasing customers for payment of overdue invoices. 'Be hard as nails with them,' she told the others. 'Be as nasty as you like. Just get the money. Every £1 overdue is making us less competitive.'

What sort of effect is this likely to have on this firm's position in the market?

_____

_____

_____

_____

> Sheila and Manjit were shelf-fillers in a supermarket. All they had to do was to re-stock shelves following detailed plans sent from head office. One day, a customer stopped and asked 'Can you tell me whereabouts the sponge fingers are, please?' The two looked at each other. Manjit just shrugged and went on shelf-filling. Sheila said 'Sorry, dunno. You'll have to ask someone else.'

What do you think they should have done, and why?

_____

_____

_____

_____

> Peter, a section manager in a factory producing packaging materials, received a phone call from Sally, one of the sales representatives. 'Peter, sorry to trouble you, but I'm with a customer and we need some information. Can you confirm a list of tensile strengths in various gauges for us?' Peter was not pleased: 'Look, young lady, I haven't got time for that sort of thing. I've got production targets to meet here. If you wanted that sort of information you should have thought about it beforehand. Goodbye.' Sally apologized to her customer as best she could: 'Sorry, we've got one or two awkward types back at the factory.'

What does this episode tell you about this company, and what effect will the incident have on its attempts to sell its products?

_____

_____

_____

_____

Danny was a service engineer for a water company and was allowed to take his van home at night. Almost every night he parked it in a spot which was very handy for him, but very inconvenient for some of his neighbours. There were numerous complaints.

Why should his employer be concerned about such a minor matter?

_____

_____

_____

_____

A marketing and customer service specialist would probably see it like this.

- Certainly, as Sarah says, poor credit control affects profitability and hence competitiveness, but a firm's credit terms are also part of its marketing mix. Customers expect credit, and many firms expect to give it. At issue here is the manner in which Sarah approaches it. The right way is to be firm but reasonable: being 'nasty' to customers is neither necessary nor helpful. It almost certainly means that some customers will go elsewhere as soon as the opportunity arises. So Sarah may be doing more harm than good to the business.

- Sheila and Manjit think that they have nothing to do with 'the marketing approach' because their job is just to fill shelves. But they are visible to customers, and customers may well ask them questions: their appearance and behaviour are both part of the firm's marketing mix. This customer will not care what their particular job is: she only knows that they represent the supermarket, and that they are unhelpful, unfriendly and lacking in knowledge. Next time she shops, it may be elsewhere. Most retail firms now expect – and train – all their staff how to respond to customers' questions, and the minimum should be to say 'Sorry, I don't know, but I'll find out for you.'

- Peter is a typical example of a production-oriented person. He needs to rethink his attitude, because if Sally can't sell Peter's output, all the production skills in the world will count for nothing. Furthermore, it is very bad practice to be unhelpful towards colleagues: the best organizations now insist not only that their customers should be treated with every consideration, but that **colleagues should be treated as customers!** Sally makes things worse, by letting the customer see that she is irritated with Peter. The customer will not be impressed with the organization and will have a lingering suspicion about its flexibility and willingness to help.

- Danny works for a company that has a local monopoly. No matter how much he annoys the neighbours, they cannot get their water from someone else. But incidents like these damage the reputation of a business. On an individual level, they may make customers more inclined to be difficult over all sorts of issues. On a public relations level, a poor reputation can lead to intense opposition to all the company's activities, from its pricing and service policies to its development proposals.

Sarah, Sheila, Manjit, Peter and Danny were not in the front line of the marketing effort. But what they did and said, and how they did and said it, had an effect on their organization's marketing mix. It is important to recognize the following.

■ All employees affect the organization's competitiveness.
■ The way you approach your job, your colleagues and your customers can either help or hinder the marketing effort.

Self-assessment 2

15 mins

1 Define what is meant by 'the marketing mix'.

_____

_____

_____

2 List **four** main elements of the marketing mix.

_____

_____

_____

_____

3 List **three** 'behind the scenes' factors that can affect long-term customer loyalty.

_____

_____

_____

Answers to these questions can be found on page 96.

6 Summary

- The marketing mix is the sum total of all the factors that make up the organization's 'offer' to its market.

- Every organization has a slightly different marketing mix; otherwise it is difficult to find a competitive edge.

- The marketing mix is made up of the 'four Ps':
  - the product;
  - the price;
  - the place and time at which the product is sold;
  - the promotional activities.

- The marketing mix affects both the customer's initial buying decision and longer-term customer satisfaction, and hence loyalty. This depends largely upon:
  - the performance of the product;
  - behind-the-scenes factors, such as efficiency, service and the attitude of the people involved.

- Maintaining a consistent quality is vital for success in the market.

- Customers prefer a reliable product from a reliable supplier.

- Customers who complain can become more loyal than before, provided their complaint is dealt with promptly and efficiently.

- The most successful market-led organizations believe that:
  - everyone on the payroll is part of the marketing mix;
  - colleagues should be treated with the same consideration as customers;
  - the way staff approach their job, their colleagues and their customers can either help or hinder the organization's marketing effort.

Session C
Analysing the market

1 Introduction

We have already seen that what counts is what the market wants, not what the supplier thinks it **ought** to want. Any organization that develops a product first, and then seeks a market for it second, is courting disaster.

So, too, is any organization that develops a product for an identified market, but then thinks it can go on producing this particular product forever. We live in a world that is constantly changing. For an organization to be successful not only today but also in the future, it must be alert to the changes that are taking place in the environment and redevelop its existing products – or produce new ones – in response to a changing market.

2 Recognizing the need for change

Managers, supervisors and team leaders in all parts of the organization need to gear their efforts to achieving this market success. This is true whether or not they are directly involved in marketing activities.

Activity 18

3 mins

How does an organization know whether its product is meeting the needs of the market? Suggest **three** different ways of finding out.

_____

_____

_____

As you saw in sessions A and B there are three main ways of knowing whether a product is meeting the needs of its market. The first is simply to look at sales (or take-up, in the case of non-commercial organizations). If sales are on target, clearly the product is meeting the needs of the market. If they are significantly above target, it would be worth finding out why, in order to be able to exploit this success further, and perhaps extend it to other products.

On the other hand, if demand for the product has not matched expectations, or if it is falling, it is not meeting the needs of the market, or not as well as it did before. If sales are stagnating, there is a question mark over the product.

This takes us on to the second source of knowledge: market research. Research can help to show why demand is changing, and whether it is likely to go on doing so.

The third main indicator of how well the product is meeting the needs of the market is feedback from customers, including distributors.

■ Positive feedback:

in the nature of things, people are more likely to complain about a product they dislike than applaud one they like, but some customers are kind enough to write or phone saying how pleased they are.

■ Negative feedback:

complaints, returns, cancellations, and similar signs of dissatisfaction.

Organizations should not be afraid of complaints. Any feedback is better than none, and knowing what customers dislike, and where problems may lie, enables them to make improvements sooner rather than later.

People often find it hard to understand why customers are not buying a particular product any longer. There is even a tendency to blame the customers: perhaps they have become less interested in quality, less loyal, even less intelligent.

Of course, this is a fundamental mistake. Change is in the market's very nature:

■ The needs of customers change.
■ The other products available in the market change.
■ All products have a limited life, even if ways are found of prolonging it.

Once an organization has realized that demand for its products or services is declining, it must first ask itself why. And once it has established why, it must consider what changes should be made to the existing product or service – or whether new customer needs are arising that call for the development of new products or services.

If you are to understand why demand has fallen – or, rather better, be able to predict when demand will fall or rise, and respond accordingly – you need to be aware of changes in the external environment. This is where what is known as 'PESTLE analysis' comes in.

3 PESTLE analysis

Carrying out a PESTLE analysis will encourage you to think about a wide range of potentially relevant factors in the external environment. These factors are:

■ political;
■ economic;
■ social;
■ technological;
■ legal;
■ environmental.

Many of these factors overlap each other. It's not always easy, for example, to decide whether a factor is political or economic. But this doesn't really matter. The main purpose of carrying out a PESTLE analysis is to get you thinking about what is happening in the external environment – and then what effect this may have on your organization.

■ **Political factors**

The government can have a major impact on organizations. It can promote the growth of businesses through policies that increase the amount of money people have to spend. Setting low inflation as a primary target, for example, encourages the Bank of England to set low interest rates. This, in turn, encourages people to borrow more and then spend more in the shops – particularly on what are called luxury goods. So manufacturers and retailers of luxury goods are able to increase their ranges and hence their profits.

A more specific example of how the government can affect organizations is its introduction of the National Lottery in 1994. The effect on Ladbrokes' betting shop business was to slash its profits by around £10 million in six months, leading to 300 people being made redundant.

■ **Economic factors**

Some developments in the economy are dictated by government policies, and in particular the measures announced in the annual budget. A cut in duty on beer, for example, will help to boost demand and lead to increased business for breweries.

Other economic developments are outside the government's control. The destruction of New York's World Trade Centre on 11 September 2001 by two planes that had been hijacked by terrorists worsened a slump in the world's stock markets, which in turn affected a huge range of businesses, from companies selling pensions to manufacturers of mobile phones.

■ **Social factors**

The composition of a country's population has a major effect on business developments. In the last decades of the 20th century, many businesses concentrated on the youth market and on providing goods and entertainment for the 'under 30s'. But with the trend for people to live longer, so causing the percentage of the population over the age of 50 to increase considerably, more businesses have begun to concentrate on addressing their needs – particularly those of people who have retired early, have a good pension and lots of leisure time. Travel companies offering luxury cruises, for example, have expanded considerably. In fact, a huge variety of businesses involved in the travel industry have developed and expanded as the population generally has adopted a lifestyle that includes more holidays abroad.

Activity 19

Lifestyles have changed in many different ways over the last ten years. What changes can you think of that have created new opportunities for businesses under the following headings:

■ Food and drink.
■ Health.
■ Leisure.

_____

_____

_____

It would be possible to come up with dozens of ideas in response to the question in Activity 19. Here are just a few.

■ Trends in the area of food and drink have included increased vegetarianism; a rising demand for organic food; an increase in Asian ingredients and dishes, such as Japanese and Thai, in both supermarkets and restaurants; and an increased demand, particularly among the young, for iced beers and sweet canned drinks containing alcohol.

■ Regarding health, there have been increases in the number of gyms, in the number and variety of alternative therapists, such as homeopaths, osteopaths, chiropractors and aromatherapists; and a growing demand for low-fat, low-salt and low-sugar convenience foods.

■ Developments in leisure have included a growing demand for café-pubs and 'super-pubs'; a growing interest in worldwide travel; increasingly complex computer games and DVDs, and – of course – the Internet.

■ **Technological factors**
Keeping up to date with the latest technology has always been essential for business success. Today, this means using computers wherever possible – be it to control manufacturing processes, keep detailed records that can be accessed immediately, make financial transactions faster, maintain the necessary levels of stock in factories or retail outlets, or speed up communication via the Internet and emails.

■ **Legal factors**
All organizations have to take account of the framework of laws and regulations within which they operate and respond accordingly. For example, with the introduction of the Environmental Protection Act in 1990, organizations were obliged to redesign processes and purchase new

equipment for disposing of waste in order to reduce pollution. For some organizations, the Act presented an opportunity to develop and sell new non-polluting technologies.

■ **Environmental factors**

As a result of increasing concern for the environment, there are many businesses, of which The Body Shop is a notable example, that have met with success on the basis of using only natural renewable ingredients. Most supermarkets now have an organic section that reflects the concern of people for the environment as well as for their health. Some also produce carrier bags made from recyclable plastic.

Activity 20 · 5 mins

Imagine you are working at Gables Hotel, which is a small rural hotel on the edge of a National Park. It has comfortable rooms, including a bar, lounge and dining room, and a well-kept garden, but it has no other amenities and it offers a very conventional menu. The hotel often has more empty rooms than its owner would like. What trends in the general environment do you think it would be wise to point out to the hotel owner?

_____

_____

_____

_____

_____

_____

There are a number of social, technological and environmental trends that you might raise – among them the growth in the over-50s market, the increase in vegetarianism and eating organic food, and the growing interest in keeping fit. There is also the demand in the business world for hotels with a business centre containing computers and so on, where meetings and team awaydays can be held in pleasant surroundings.

What is apparent is that the hotel owners not only need to consider developments in the general environment – they also need to decide which group, or groups, of customers it might focus on in the future. Its potential market can, in fact, be broken down into a number of segments, including wealthy older people, fitness enthusiasts, vegetarians, business people, and so on.

4 Market segmentation

Most markets can be broken down into segments. These are distinct slices of the market that demand different things from a particular product range.

4.1 Segmentation and product range

The market for cars is a good example: all cars are basically self-powered boxes for moving people from place to place. However, within the car market there are many distinct needs. Retired people, managing directors, sales reps, first-time buyers, farmers, families and commuters all look for something slightly different. They represent distinct segments of the market. Segmentation is also to do with spending power: what people can afford to buy (and therefore the 'demand' they generate) depends to a large extent on their income. In most markets, there are three broad segments based on income, like this.

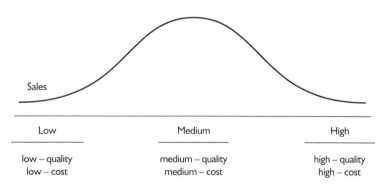

Market segmentation

As you can see from the 'distribution curve' in this diagram, the biggest sales (for most consumer products at any rate) are in the middle ranges, and this is where competition is also highest, because the total sums of money involved here are much greater.

But there is a market at the top end too; this segment produces fewer sales in total, but a relatively high cash income. Profits may also be relatively high here. There is also a market at the bottom end.

Segmentation is a reality. Organizations respond by tailoring their products to these segments. This may involve developing a wide product range that mirrors a wide range of market segments. Thus, Ford offers a wide range of cars, from small 'economy' models to large luxurious ones, and including 'people movers' and off-road vehicles. Many firms prefer to concentrate their efforts on specific sectors: the Italian firm Lamborghini only operates in the top end of the luxury segment, while Fiat concentrates on the lower and middle segments.

We can see the same process of matching the product range to market segments in a service industry like the restaurant trade.

Restaurant	Description	Market segment
'Le Chapeau Noir'	One of the top restaurants in the country, offering a wide range of individually prepared dishes cooked by internationally famous chefs. Situated in a pleasant rural location and with a very high standard of service.	**Top of the range:** ■ top quality; ■ maximum choice; ■ high prices; ■ small market.
'The Merry Chef'	Part of a nationwide chain, which offers a standardized menu at moderate prices and is organized for maximum cost-efficiency. Situated mainly in busy town centres and providing a medium level of service.	**Middle of the range:** ■ middle quality; ■ limited choice; ■ competitive prices; ■ large market.
'Sid's Cafe'	A family-run café/snack bar, offering tea, coffee and fried meals of the bacon-egg-sausage-chips-and-peas type. Situated on the edge of an industrial estate.	**Bottom of the range:** ■ low quality; ■ limited choice; ■ low prices; ■ small market.

Activity 21

5 mins

The three different restaurants are clearly aimed at three different market segments, in that they aim to attract three entirely different types of customer. How would you describe the three different types of customer?

Le Chapeau Noir

_____

_____

The Merry Chef

_____

_____

Sid's Cafe

_____

_____

One way of looking at the differences is by social class. Sid's clientele are likely to be working class; the top-of-the-range restaurant attracts the upper class; and the Merry Chef Inn is in between.

The advertising and marketing industry is interested in these distinctions, because what can be marketed successfully to one cannot necessarily be marketed to the others. In the past the industry often referred to these groups by a letter.

A   professionals;
B   managers and other senior grades;
C1   white collar workers;
C2   skilled manual workers;
D   unskilled manual workers.

However, this is a very crude division, and nowadays consumers are usually analysed in more sensitive ways, for example:

■ by the area in which they live (for example through the Area Classification of Residential Neighbourhood or ACORN system);
■ according to their tastes, interests and lifestyles (e.g. by finding out which newspapers they read, the type of holidays they take and the kind of cars they drive).

Either way, the two principal respects in which the segments differ are:

- the amount they have available to spend;
- their needs in terms of quality.

Some restaurants are capable of competing in more than one segment of the market. Many Chinese restaurants, for example, have three different products aimed at three distinct segments within the market for Chinese meals.

- The basic low-cost 'business lunch' for working people in a hurry.
- The full-menu evening meal, a more leisurely affair with a higher standard of service and 'trimmings'.
- The take-away and home delivery service.

So Chinese restaurants have a product range that consists of three products. Note that 'product' refers to the type of meal, not the individual items a customer buying a meal will actually choose from.

Activity 22

2 mins

Why is it to the advantage of a restaurant to compete in three separate market segments rather than just one? Note down **one** good reason.

_____

_____

_____

_____

Working in several market segments is also a matter of spreading risk. If an organization meets problems in one segment and makes a loss, there is a good chance that the others will still produce enough profit to keep the business afloat.

It is a simple matter of economics. Restaurants have a particular set of resources – human skills, equipment etc. If they can utilize these same resources across three market segments instead of one, they are both increasing their revenue and reducing their unit costs. It is far more profitable than concentrating on just one part of the market. The same is true of almost any sector of the market. However, where the segments in a market differ greatly, firms may prefer to concentrate on the segments where they have expertise. Rolls-Royce is unlikely to try to enter the market segment that buys cheap run-abouts.

4.2 Range and choice

Simple economics is not the only reason for offering a range of products; it is also important to be able to offer customers a choice. Often this means providing relatively minor variations within each product in the range, as in the case of the Chinese restaurant.

For another example, take a confectionery wholesaler that distributes its products to high street retailers.

To persuade the retailers to do business with them, the wholesaler must be able to offer what the retailers believe their market wants. In this case, it is variety: a range of different brands, types, flavours, colours and sizes from which to choose.

Retailers will insist on the wholesaler supplying the full range of products and maintaining their availability at all times. This will have a big impact on the way the wholesaler approaches its business, and in turn on the manufacturers from which it acquires its supplies.

Customers nearly always appreciate being offered a choice of products. Few, for example, would want to go to a car show-room and not be offered a choice of engine sizes, colours, finishes and accessories.

Even in business markets, such as for office furniture, computers, catering services and packaging materials, the customer appreciates being offered a choice and is unlikely to be impressed by suppliers who do not offer it.

But giving the customers the choice they demand can be hard work for people throughout the supplying organization. It usually means:

Choice is a key concept in consumer marketing. Even when we buy something as ordinary as a dustbin, we like to have a choice of colours, sizes, shapes and materials. The shop that can offer us the biggest range is more likely to see the colour of our money.

- developing a range of lines – and thus more time and money spent on research, design, scheduling, setting up machines, training people and so on;
- maintaining a range of stock and a variety of facilities – and thus more time and money spent on warehousing, keeping inventory records, recording stock movements and other overheads.

Activity 23

20 mins

S/NVQs A1.3, D1.1

This activity may provide the basis of appropriate evidence for your S/NVQ portfolio. If you are intending to take this course of action, it might be better to write your answers on separate sheets of paper.

Think about the range of products (or one of the ranges, if there are several) that your own organization offers. These will be products of a similar type, but aimed at different segments of the market, and will draw on the same basic skills and other resources. Analyse the range in terms of price and quality.

1   Arrange them in order from low quality/price through to high quality/price. If there is a large number, choose **not more than five** that represent distinct price/quality levels.

2   Note down what kinds of customers each product in the range is expected to sell to. (You may need to consult whoever specializes in marketing about this.) This will establish what market segments each product is aimed at.

3   Research some price and sales or uptake figures for the range of products you have identified.

   ■ Average sale price for each product.
   ■ Average number of units sold per month (or per quarter or per year, if more convenient).
   ■ Average gross profit margin for each product.

4   Calculate:

   a   the total sales value;
   b   the total gross profit that each product returns on average in the period you have chosen.

5   Present some of your figures graphically:

   ■ Pie charts showing:
      a   each product's share of total sales by unit;
      b   each product's share of total gross profit.
   ■ A chart showing average number of units by sales price per unit.

When you have done all this, consider what you have learned about the way market segmentation works in your organization. Are there any gaps in the range? Where is demand biggest? Are there products in the range that are generating so little activity that they may not be worthwhile?

Try to discuss these issues with someone who has marketing or financial responsibilities. What is the thinking behind the range as it presently stands. What plans, if any, are there to change it? What suggestions for improvement can you contribute?

In completing the last activity you will have begun to think about the areas in which your organization is strongest and those where it is weakest. You will, in fact, have taken the first steps to completing what is known as a SWOT analysis.

5 SWOT analysis

SWOT stands for:

- strengths;
- weaknesses;
- opportunities;
- threats.

A SWOT analysis is a valuable tool for all managers because it helps them to understand the nature of the organization they work for and to identify possible ways of moving forward in the future. It can act as a springboard for change and help a manager in deciding on possible objectives for a marketing plan.

A SWOT analysis is usually set out in a box divided into four sections, each of which contains a number of points about an organization – or just part of an organization. Exactly what these points are will depend on the nature of the organization, as you can see here.

Strengths	**Weaknesses**
The things it does well	The things it does badly
Resources	Lack of certain resources
Staff skills	Gaps in skills
Possibly high staff morale	Possibly low staff morale
High demand for its products/services	Low demand for its products/services
Possibly its financial situation	Possibly its financial situation
Opportunities	**Threats**
National or local trends that point to a growing demand for a new or existing product	National or local trends that may reduce demand for existing product
	Other providers of the product that may take away customers

To see how carrying out a SWOT analysis can work out in practice, let's return to the example of Gables Hotel, which was described briefly in Activity 20. You have already identified a few trends in the general environment that the hotel owners ought to start thinking about. Do any of these trends represent opportunities for the hotel? What are the hotel's strengths, which will enable it to respond positively to these opportunities? And what are the weaknesses that it should address if it is not to succumb to the various threats posed by the outside world?

SWOT analysis for Gables Hotel

Strengths	Weaknesses
Provides well-decorated, centrally heated, clean and comfortable rooms	Small choice of meals on daily menu and not as good as those provided by pub in local village – lack of culinary skills
Staff know about customer care and provide a prompt and courteous service to guests	No amenities for guests on rainy days, apart from lounge
Generally high morale	No regular customer base and hotel often less than half full
The local countryside is a great attraction	
Value of property considerably higher than price paid by present owners	
Opportunities	**Threats**
Growing demand for restaurants that provide organic and local produce and vegetarian dishes	Pub in local village renowned for quality of its food
Growing demand for fitness and sporting facilities	Hotel a few miles away has begun to offer 'bargain weekends' outside the high season
Demand for business centres – with computers and access to Internet – in pleasant surroundings	

Activity 24 · · 5 mins

On the basis of the SWOT analysis for Gables Hotel, what do you think is the best way forward for the hotel? What actions might it take to increase its business?

_____

_____

_____

The hotel is worth rather more than the owners paid for it, which suggests that they can borrow some money to pay for some improvements. A few cheap improvements to take advantage of the fitness trend would be to purchase bicycles for use by guests and employ the services of local guide for walking tours. Far more expensive would be to have a small gym built. Another possible investment would be to set up a business centre, with computers, printers, photocopiers, scanner and fax machines, and access to the Internet. The hotel could also employ a good chef with the ability to improve the quality of the food it offers, and perhaps make a feature of using organic and local ingredients and providing a range of vegetarian meals. Of course, once all these improvements have been made, the hotel will have to set about promoting itself. If it decides, for example, to create a business centre, it will need to promote itself to business as an ideal venue for meetings and team awaydays.

Activity 25

What do you see as the strengths and weaknesses of the organization you work for? And what are the opportunities and threats? Have a go at doing a SWOT analysis for your organization. Alternatively, just focus on your department and do a SWOT analysis for this.

6 The marketing plan

Once an organization has carried out a SWOT analysis, it can start thinking about drawing up a marketing plan. Such a plan usually consists of the following items.

- Background – brief description of the organization and its present market.
- Organization's mission statement – i.e. a statement of the long-term purpose of the organization.
- Outline of general environmental trends – PESTLE analysis.
- Outline of organization's specific environment – customers and competitors.
- SWOT analysis.

- Strategic objectives – i.e. a statement of the long-term objectives outlining the direction in which it is intended the organization should go. The objectives should:
  - build on the organization's strengths;
  - turn its weaknesses into strengths;
  - make the most of opportunities;
  - plan around the threats.
- Key policies on the four Ps:
  - product;
  - price;
  - place;
  - promotion.
- Outline of how and when policies are to be put into practice.

Several of these items have already been discussed in this workbook. In the next session we are going to return to the four Ps – in particular, price, place and promotion.

Self assessment 3

15 mins

1   Fill in the missing words in this statement.

Signs that a product is meeting the needs of the market are:

sales or take-up are on or above _____;

the number of approving letters or phone calls from _____ goes up;

there is a low number of _____.

2   What are the six different types of factors or trends that a PESTLE analysis is concerned with?

P _____

E _____

S _____

T _____

L _____

E _____

3   Explain what is meant by a segment of the market.

_____

_____

_____

4   In a SWOT analysis, what do the letters S, W, O and T stand for?

S _____

W _____

O _____

T _____

5   Why is a SWOT analysis an important part of a marketing plan?

_____

_____

_____

Answers to these questions can be found on page 96.

7 Summary

- All products have a limited life-cycle, but their useful life can be prolonged.

- To understand why demand for a product has fallen – or, rather better, be able to predict when demand will fall or rise, and respond accordingly – you need to be aware of changes in the external environment.

- Carrying out a PESTLE analysis will help you to identify the full range of trends and factors in the external environment that your organization needs to take into account. These are political, economic, social, technological, legal and environmental.

- Most organizations try to offer a range of products to the market. This brings in extra revenues by using the same basic skills and material resources.

- The range of products is designed to match different segments of the market, which are defined mainly by:
  - the amount they have to spend;
  - their needs in terms of quality.

- All things being equal, customers tend to prefer the supplier who offers them the widest choice. This is another reason for offering a range of products.

- A SWOT analysis is a valuable tool for all managers because it helps them to understand the nature of the organization they work for and to identify changes that the organization might make to its products in the future.

- SWOT stands for strengths, weaknesses, opportunities and threats.

- The strengths and weaknesses are factors within the organization itself.

- The opportunities and threats come from the general environment – and every organization needs to respond to them if it is to continue meeting customer needs and stay in business.

Session D
Getting the price, place and promotion right

1 Introduction

In Session B we focused on what is involved on getting the product right – and how you might contribute to this as a manger. In this session we turn to the three other Ps: price, place (including time), and promotion.

Suppose you have the right product, but you offer it to the market at too high a price or a year late (or, just as bad, a year early). Obviously, you will miss the boat.

On the other hand, suppose you have the right product, at the right price, but you launch it, say, in East Anglia only, when the real market is the whole of Northern Europe. Again, you will miss the boat.

These two suppositions may be extreme, but it is surprising how often organizations fail to hit the right price, place and time for their products. There may be all sorts of reasons for this, from failure to study the market accurately, to development problems, to sheer bad luck. Added to this, the organization may fail to promote the product effectively. The upshot is a disaster.

In this session you will find out more about why the right price, place, time and promotion are so crucial, and look at some of the things that organizations – and that means the people in them – can do to make sure things go right.

2 The right price

Have you ever been to a supermarket and found that the product you want to buy is not available because it's on special offer and so has been snapped up by other customers? The product may not be a particularly good one, but if two are offered for the price of one you can be sure that stocks will run out very quickly.

In principle, anything will sell (i.e. there will be demand for anything) if the price falls low enough. Scrap metal is a case in point. Even a rusty and broken-down washing machine, which will never work again, can be sold as scrap for a small sum.

The problem with most goods and services is that the price has to be low enough to create a demand, but high enough to produce a profit, and it is difficult to get this right.

2.1 Costing a product

To produce a profit, the price of a product must produce a revenue that is greater than the total costs involved in getting it to the customer.

Activity 26 · 5 mins

Grindleford Toys have many product groups, including high-quality, cast-metal miniature toys. From the initial idea stage to distribution, many different costs go into a product such as this. List six of them.

_____

_____

_____

_____

_____

The main costs associated with a manufactured product are generally as follows:

- Development costs, including:

  - market research;
  - design and pre-production costs;
  - making dies and jigs;
  - test-runs.

- Direct production costs, including:

  - set-up costs;
  - materials (metal, paint, rubber);
  - components bought in;
  - packaging;
  - repairs and maintenance to machinery etc.;
  - wages and salaries of production staff;
  - energy.

- Indirect (overhead) costs, including:

  - management costs;
  - administrative costs (including wages and salaries of office staff);
  - rent, rates etc.;
  - lighting, heating etc.;
  - telephone, post, couriers etc.;
  - insurance, legal fees etc.;
  - training.

- Distribution and selling costs, including:

  - storage and transport costs;
  - advertising and costs of promotional events;
  - promotional literature;
  - salaries of selling staff;
  - travel and other expenses.

There may be many more incidental costs than I have listed, and there also has to be a margin for profit; and probably something for tax.

The simplest way to work out the price of a product is to add up all the anticipated costs and then add a percentage for profit. (The costing of service products is broadly similar, except that materials and 'production' costs are usually insignificant, while labour costs are considerably higher.)

This is the so-called 'cost-plus' method. However, this method is based entirely on internal considerations, especially production; it takes no account whatsoever of the market.

4.2 Pricing for the market

Unfortunately for Grindleford Toys, they are facing lower-priced competition from China, and in the last few years they have seen a gradual, but steady, decline in the demand for their cars. They decide that one solution might be to produce a new model. They work out that a new model aimed at the middle segment of the market will cost £4.20 to make, on a production run of 10,000. If they add 15% as a profit margin, this will bring the price at which it can be supplied to retailers to £4.83. Retailers will then add their own margin, and the model will probably appear in the shops at £5.99.

Activity 27   3 mins

> This is the Japanese approach, which proved so successful from the 1960s onwards: find out what the market wants, and what it is prepared to pay, then produce a product at that price. Since competition is expected to grow every year, every part of the organization is expected to find cost reductions and productivity gains that will maintain or improve the competitive position. The key is continuous improvement of process quality – an approach known in Japan as *Kaizen*, which is becoming widely accepted throughout the world.

Perhaps this is not the right price for the product. What other considerations will Grindleford's have to bear in mind when setting a price? Try to think of **two**.

_____

_____

_____

_____

The price may be right from Grindleford's point of view, but is it right for the market? They need to consider how it compares with the prices of competing products. If the competition sells at £4.99, how can this product sell at £5.99?

A market-led firm will approach this from a different angle: 'At what price can we sell this product? OK, now how can we produce the product at that price?'

If the answer is 'We can't', then it is a waste of time and money even trying.

Activity 28

3 mins

There is no reason in principle why Grindleford's products should not sell, at a higher price, in the top segment of the market, provided they are right for that segment. What would 'right' be in this context?

_____

_____

_____

_____

A product that survives in the upper end of the market must have something about it that justifies the higher price, for example:

- superior quality and durability;
- a high reputation and a quality brand name;
- superior style and fashion.

So, with the right match between product quality and price, Grindleford Toys can succeed. However, they can still fail if they don't pay sufficient attention to distribution and don't identify the retailers who are most likely to sell their toys. In other words, it is essential that they consider 'place'.

3 The right place

Perhaps you had cereal for breakfast today, or perhaps a cup of coffee and a slice of toast. Whatever it was, it's unlikely that you produced these things yourself. The raw materials probably came from overseas, perhaps from the other side of the globe, and even the factory that processed them may have been hundreds of miles away. In order for you to buy them, they had to be brought to a place where you could conveniently do so. The same applies to the customers who buy the products that we ourselves supply.

Two hundred years ago, people in countries like Britain were fairly self-sufficient. Their needs were simple – mainly food, clothing and basic tools and equipment – and most they could either produce themselves or get from a fairly local source. Now our needs are much more complex and we produce very little for our own direct use. The way we live is utterly dependent on worldwide markets and a system of distribution that brings us what we demand from the ends of the earth if necessary.

Making sure that goods and services are available when the customer wants to buy them is part of marketing, and comes under the general heading of **distribution**.

You can think of distribution in two main ways:

■ the chain of distribution;
■ physical distribution.

These obviously refer to goods rather than services, but the distribution of service products is similarly important. So too is the storage and handling of the stocks prior to delivery.

3.1 The chain of distribution

The 'chain of production and distribution' looks like this.

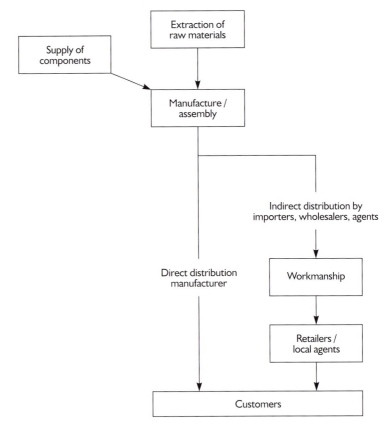

Chain of distribution

This chain may have few links or many, but if even one of them fails, the customer's needs will not be met, and he or she will go elsewhere.

3.2 Stock handling and storage

Since warehousing plays an important part in the chain of distribution, the efficiency of stock handling and storage obviously affects the ability to supply the right product at the right place and time.

Here is an example of what can go wrong.

Mary, the supervisor in an office equipment company, received an order for a white leather executive chair, reference number 2140. She checked with the stock records, which showed one such chair in stock.

Mary passed the order down to the warehouse supervisor, who phoned back to say that bin 2140 was empty. As the order was for urgent delivery, the customer cancelled it.

Later that day, Mary was walking through the warehouse on her way to the canteen, when she spotted what she thought was a white leather chair type 2140 perched on top of a bin containing desks. She had a word with one of the warehouse staff, who explained that a colleague had put the chair there three weeks previously because bin 2140 was full at the time.

Activity 29

3 mins

What was the problem in this case, and who was responsible?

_____

_____

_____

_____

_____

_____

The problem was lack of communication – the warehouse staff didn't communicate what they had done. But the responsibility was the warehouse supervisor's:

- for not ensuring that his staff realized they needed to communicate about such things;
- perhaps for not encouraging an atmosphere in which people were willing to communicate;
- and certainly for not carrying out spot checks on bin contents.

This incident illustrates just some of the problems of place and time which arise every day in the handling, storage and control of stock. The supervisor is often the person best able to solve these problems.

It's no good producing the right product at the right price, if we cannot get it to the customer at the right time.

3.3 Physical distribution

Then there is the transport side, the physical distribution: the process of sending the products down the chain from one location to another, until they reach the customer.

Physical delivery of the product is an extremely important part of the marketing mix. Indeed, under contract law, the buyer has the right to make delivery terms a condition of the contract; and if the delivery is late, they can refuse payment and even sue for damages. Moreover, you're likely to lose that customer to another supplier.

In recent years, customers' delivery needs have tightened up. Many manufacturers and retailers now operate a 'just-in-time' system for deliveries of goods. This means that the goods should be timed to arrive just before they are needed, no later, and never much earlier. Thus, supermarkets expect that delivery vans will arrive at a particular time, so that their staff can be ready to check the goods and move them straight onto the shelves on the shop floor.

Manufacturers expect parts and sub-assemblies to arrive precisely when they are needed on the assembly line.

Activity 30 · 4 mins

What do you think is the main advantage of the just-in-time system to retailers and manufacturers?

_____

_____

_____

The principal advantage for the customer is having to hold only a very small amount of stock. Stock costs money, and it needs space to house it and people to look after it. It also ties up money until the moment when the stock is actually sold.

Activity 31 · 3 mins

What disadvantages does a just-in-time delivery system have for the supplier? Write down **two** suggestions.

_____

_____

Next time you are in a large supermarket, sneak a look into the stock room. You'll find that it's surprisingly small. Supermarkets store their stock on the shelves: their aim is to sell it, not warehouse it. The stock room is mainly used for storing 'faulty returns', goods delivered in error and extra stocks required for special promotions.

Customers such as supermarkets work long hours and have a high throughput, and they may require deliveries to be made at any time of day or night. This means that the supplier's staff, and especially despatch staff and drivers, also have to match these hours, which may be inconvenient for them.

It also means that, in effect, the supplier does the warehousing for the customer, and thus carries the cost of that operation.

Third, the system means more frequent and generally smaller deliveries, because the customer is no longer prepared to store more than a minimum of stock.

Suppliers often grumble about all this, but at the end of the day they have no choice. There is always competition, and if one supplier cannot, or will not, deliver at the right place and the right time, then someone else certainly will.

Meeting delivery needs within the narrow time-frame often demanded calls for hard work and attention to detail.

> Samuelsons produce hot pre-packed meals, which they distribute to offices, shops and factories over a wide area, using a small fleet of vans. Orders are accepted up to 11 am on the day they are required, and all orders are delivered by arrangement between 12 noon and 2 pm.

Activity 32

5 mins

Jot down **four** of the things that Samuelsons would have to do to make sure that their customers got what they wanted at the right time and place. (Don't worry about the product itself – you can assume they have got the raw materials, equipment and so on.)

_____

_____

_____

_____

All sorts of things could go wrong with a time-sensitive operation like this. Some of the most important areas are as follows.

■ Ensure that all orders have correct consignment notes so that they go to the right address.
■ Double-check that each consignment is actually what the customer ordered.
■ Make sure the orders are properly packed so that they don't get spilled or contaminated.
■ Plan the most effective routes for the vehicles.
■ Make sure the drivers are properly trained and instructed.
■ Make sure the vehicles are regularly serviced and repaired so as to minimize the risk of breakdowns.

- Make sure the vehicles meet legal requirements so that they aren't kept off the road unnecessarily.
- Make sure there is a vehicle and driver on stand-by in case of emergencies.

Similar points will apply to almost any organization which operates a distribution service. All these things need to be done by the people behind the scenes in order to support the marketing operation. The market demands a service that is economical, but also reliable; customers soon get tired of receiving their orders late or not at all!

3.4 Distribution of services

Service-based organizations are not necessarily concerned with distributing goods; but they do have to make sure that the service they offer is 'delivered' to the customer. A local authority, for example, needs to ensure that its services are made available to everyone in the area for which it is responsible, and that they can gain access to it with the minimum of difficulty.

Activity 33 · 5 mins

Wetlands District Council's customers are the people who live and work in the district. It provides them with numerous services, such as refuse collection, street lighting, road maintenance, council housing, care homes and schools.

What would be involved in making a service like advice for council tenants available at the right place and time? Write down **two** or **three** suggestions.

_____

_____

_____

_____

_____

The first issue is informing the customers that the service exists. This is much harder than one might imagine. Even when it is something that would be to people's advantage, it takes a big commitment of time, money and energy to push 'awareness' beyond the 50% level.

The next step is to make it easy for the customers to gain access to the service. In recent years, councils have tried to achieve this by such means as:

- providing free telephone 'advice-lines' for use by the public;
- offering advice outside normal hours, for example in the evening and at weekends;
- breaking up the housing department into smaller units and siting these locally, near where the tenants actually live;
- fitting out lorries or buses as mobile advice centres and touring the localities on pre-advertised dates;
- sending council officers to visit people in their homes.

This sort of thing is not yet universal, but it is a clear sign that local authorities and similar organizations are adopting a marketing approach towards the services they supply.

4 The right time

Right for the customer, that is. This may or may not correspond with 'as soon as we can do it without disruption to our usual way of doing things'.

4.1 'I want it now!'

Time often gives one supplier the competitive edge.

> Commercial markets plan ahead and usually seek fixed dates for delivery well in advance. Early delivery is often a nuisance rather than a benefit. Consumer markets are different. Customers often want their new purchase instantly and feel frustrated if this isn't possible. Anyone who has ever ordered a three-piece suite will know the feeling.

Ramiz wanted to buy a new computer. This is how he decided between the twenty or so possible suppliers.

- He worked out the exact specifications he wanted.
- He listed the suppliers who could provide exactly that.
- He checked the prices by telephone and shortlisted three.
- He then checked how soon they could deliver and chose the quickest.

All other things being equal, the time factor gave one supplier the competitive edge (and indeed the computer arrived exactly when they promised). This firm was well-managed and well-organized, and everyone working there gave top priority to the customer's needs: that's why it got the business.

Activity 34

5 mins

Wetlands District Council was seeking tenders for the installation of a new computer system in its main offices. It shortlisted three different suppliers.

Supplier A was cheap, but would need 'about nine months' to complete the installation. Supplier B was mid-priced, and would also need nine months to complete the installation, but gave a cast-iron guarantee that the work would be completed on time. Supplier C was more expensive, but offered to complete the work in seven months.

Which one would you choose, all other things being equal? Give the reasons for your choice.

_____

_____

_____

_____

A difficult choice, because we do not know how much weight this customer would place on time as opposed to money. On the whole, the best choice is probably Supplier B, because it is better to be sure about completion **within a given time** than **unsure** about a somewhat earlier time.

Harry was quality control supervisor on a production line making speakers for sound systems. One day the sales manager came in and told him that batch number 9193 (fifty pairs of speakers for export) must be ready by 4 pm the following day, as they had to be delivered to the airport six hours later. (This was three whole days ahead of the normal schedule.)

When the sales manager had gone, Harry said to Joyce, his line manager, 'Sales have gone and done it again, Joyce. All they do is promise customers ridiculous deadlines, and to hell with everything else.'

Activity 35   4 mins

We've all heard comments like Harry's. What points would you make to Harry if you were Joyce? Write your thoughts down in **one** or **two** sentences.

_____

_____

_____

_____

_____

_____

An agreed delivery date is almost always a condition of an order, and sometimes it is the most important condition. Sometimes it is impossible to get the order without being prepared to offer an ultra-short lead time.

Of course, it is always possible for the sales team simply to tell their customer, 'Sorry – we can't do it in the time. It'll mean messing up our routine.' But that is a very plain message to the customer that their order isn't important enough to bother with: next time that customer will go elsewhere.

4.2 Seasonality

The need to supply products at the right time affects the way work is organized, especially where demand fluctuates through the year.

Activity 36

5 mins

John sells soap powder, Mary sells children's toys. What do you think will be the biggest difference between their working lives?

_____

_____

There are several differences you might have written down – for example, toys are a varied and rapidly changing product group, while the range of soap powder is limited and remains much the same year in year out.

The biggest difference, though, is 'seasonality'. Soap powder sales are only slightly seasonal, dipping a little in the summer months. John will therefore have a steady routine that will not vary much from month to month. Children's toys, on the other hand, are highly seasonal: almost 60% of all retail toy sales take place in the pre-Christmas period.

> Much industrial and commercial activity is seasonally 'skewed'. Think about: electricity generation; agricultural contracting; hotels; holiday companies; estate agencies (spring is the busiest time for house sales); construction (winter is a relatively quiet period).

This means that Mary's activities will be quite different at different times of year. She will probably be extremely busy:

- in January, when the major toy fairs take place and the big retailers are placing their orders for the following Christmas;
- in the middle of the year, when the smaller retailers are placing Christmas orders.

For the rest of the year, pressure of work will be much lower.

Seasonal demand will also influence the way manufacturers organize their work. Anyone who makes seasonal products is likely to find themselves under a great deal of pressure at certain peak times. But it's essential to meet the challenge: otherwise, yet again, a competitor will do so.

Activity 37 · 6 mins

Write down a list of **ten** consumer products for which demand is highly seasonal.

_____   _____

_____   _____

_____   _____

_____   _____

_____   _____

Suggestions to this Activity can be found on page 98.

A vast variety of goods (and services – for example, restaurants offering facilities for Christmas) fall into the category of seasonal products, and market research plus experience will tell those concerned quite clearly when the peaks are to be expected. However, there can still be unpredictable surges (or slumps) in demand, plus special priority orders. In the face of fierce competition, it is essential to get the product to its destination on time – and the person who decides what is meant by 'on time' is the customer!

5 The right promotion

Promotion is the 'sharp end' of the marketing process. In fact, these are the activities that most people think of first when they hear the word 'marketing'. Of course, marketing is a much wider concept, but that does not diminish the importance of promotion.

We may well deliver the right product at the right price to the right place at the right time, but it will not be alone in that marketplace. Skilful competitors will have their own products there, and their marketing mix, though no doubt different from ours, is also designed to be attractive to the customer.

At this stage, the last competitive edge that we have is the skill and initiative of our promotional and selling people.

The AIDA strategy

EXTENSION 3
Promotion is a specialized subject outside the scope of this workbook. If you would like to learn more about it, try reading N. Robinson's *Marketing Tool Kit*.

In broad terms, both promotion and selling follow the AIDA strategy. This stands for the processes involved in persuading the customer to buy our product rather than another by:

getting their **A**ttention;
arousing their **I**nterest in the product;
stimulating a **D**esire to acquire it;
turning desire into **A**ction, i.e. a purchase.

The AIDA strategy involves four types of activity:

- advertising;
- sales promotion;
- public relations;
- selling.

5.1 Advertising, sales promotion and public relations

Adverts appear in newspapers and magazines, on TV and the radio, on websites, on hoardings in streets and stations, on and inside taxis, buses and trains, in the Yellow Pages – the list goes on and on. No doubt you could describe dozens of adverts – but how many of them have had an influence on what you buy?

Activity 38 · 10 mins

Briefly describe three adverts for a product that you could afford to buy. In each case make a note of whether the effect of the advert was to persuade you to buy a particular product brand – for example, one brand of jeans rather than another. Or did you think the advert had no effect at all?

Advert 1:

_____

_____

Effect:

_____

Advert 2:

_____

_____

Effect:

_____

Advert 3:

_____

_____

Effect:

_____

It would not be unusual to find that an advert had not persuaded you to buy a particular product. In fact, not all advertising is about persuasion. Sometimes it is mainly about informing or reminding people about a product.

Forms of advertising

Information advertising is used when a new product is developed and there is a need to build a demand for it – as, for example, when mobile phones or DVD players were first introduced to the market. In contrast, reminder advertising is used for unique products that have been around a long time – as in the case of Coca-Cola.

Persuasive advertising is used when several companies are competing for the same market. Sometimes, persuasion can take the form of a comparison – as when washing powder adverts compare clothes washed in two different powders.

Go back to the three adverts you described in Activity 38. Do you think the purpose of any of them was to inform or remind, rather than persuade?

Direct mail

Closely related to advertising is direct mail. Whether through the post or the Internet, this tries to get the customer to respond directly:

- by making a purchase;
- or by requesting further information (this is a means of introducing a sales person into the equation).

Sales promotion

Many different techniques are directed at potential customers that are designed to create interest, generate enquiries and encourage sales. There is a huge variety of techniques, all working on the proposition that people find it difficult to resist anything that looks like a 'bargain'. They include:

- money-off vouchers;
- competitions;
- gifts and other 'offers' that involve collecting and sending in labels, tokens etc;
- 'buy five, get the sixth free' offers.

An example of a company employing sales promotion techniques very effectively is the Japanese company, Akai. In India it persuaded people to buy its colour TV sets by offering a good trade-in price for black and white TVs, or offering a free radio, watch or calculator with a new TV. But in the long run, sales promotions of this type are not always effective. After a while they can, in fact, result in consumers never buying a product except when it is on 'special offer'. Generally speaking, advertising is more likely than sales promotions to establish long-term customers who remain loyal to a particular brand of product.

Public relations

Public relations is all about promoting or protecting the image of an organization or of its products. Most large organizations have a PR department whose main function is to monitor public opinion about the organization and distribute information that will persuade existing and potential customers that this is a good organization to buy from.

Many things contribute to an organization's image – from the appearance of its premises and the way its staff answer the phone, to activities that it undertakes in the community, such as making donations to local schools or youth groups, or a cultural festival. Public relations staff aim to build up a good image by presenting news about the organization – whether through national or local newspapers, or the Internet – in a positive light.

Public relations staff also help to sell new products by publicizing them in a number of ways other than advertising. A good example of this was Microsoft's campaign to launch Windows 95. By the launch date in August 1995, no paid-for advertisements had appeared. But everyone knew about the product because so many stories had appeared in the press – 6,852 stories over less than eight weeks according to the *Wall Street Journal*. At a price of 90 dollars, by the end of the first week US sales were 108 million dollars.

Activity 39 · 45 mins

S/NVQs D1.1, A1.3

This Activity may provide the basis of appropriate evidence for your S/NVQ portfolio. If you are intending to take this course of action, it might be better to write your answers on separate sheets of paper.

Select one of your organization's new/recent products.

First, find out about the period when it was first launched. What was done in terms of the following.

1   Advertising:

    how much, where, when, and at what cost?

2   Sales promotion:

    what techniques were used?

3   Public relations:

    what techniques were used?

Second, get a view from those responsible on how effective each of these three parts of the marketing effort was.

Third, write up your ideas for improvements to the advertising, promotion and public relations approach used.

If you are compiling an S/NVQ portfolio, it would be useful to add examples of advertisements, promotional and public relations materials with comments attached.

> Sales promotions often feature a 'free gift' or other benefit in addition to the item purchased. Of course, sellers try to minimize the cost of any such attraction to themselves, while exaggerating its 'value' to the customer. One notorious exception was the promotion launched by Hoover in the early 1990s. Hoover offered free flights to the USA with every appliance purchased. Sales boomed, but the demand for the free flights was almost as big. The cost – and the multitude of wrangles with customers as Hoover tried to get it under control – came close to bankrupting the company.

5.2 Selling – the retail sector

Many of us may think of selling as a specialist role, about which the rest of us don't have to worry too much. Perhaps this is true in some organizations, but there are many cases – of which retailing is an obvious example – where it isn't.

Nearly one employed person in every eight works in retailing, and many of them are directly involved in selling.

Of course selling in the retail sector takes different forms.

- Some retail sales staff are expected to **sell actively**, by going up to every customer who enters and working through a sales routine.
- Others are told not to approach customers, but when a customer asks them for help, they are expected to 'close the sale', **encourage** them to buy extra items ('add-on sales') or buy a higher-priced alternative ('selling up').
- The majority of retail staff do not sell actively, but are expected to **make it easier for customers to buy** by being polite, helpful and informative.

Obviously, supervisors have a key role to play in all three situations, because they are responsible for giving a good example and making sure that the sales staff perform their selling tasks effectively.

> Overall the most important form of selling used in retailing does not involve sales staff at all. It is the way the goods are displayed in order to make them as attractive and desirable as possible. This speciality is called merchandising, or, alternatively, 'silent selling'.

Activity 40 5 mins

If you have never worked in retailing you may not have realized that these different selling strategies existed, but if you think about your own experiences as a shopper, you will soon recognize them. Try to give **one** example of each of the following types of retail firm.

In Type 1, staff sell actively by approaching customers.

_____

In Type 2, staff sell, but only after customers approach them.

_____

In Type 3, staff only have to help customers buy.

_____

Some examples can be found on page 98.

5.3 Selling – the salesforce method

EXTENSION 4
For more about the role of the sales force and effective selling see Extension 4

But what about all those organizations where the selling is done by sales representatives who go 'out on the road'? Many people sell gas or electricity services, or double glazing, directly to consumers, but the bulk of the professional representatives work for the industrial, commercial and service sectors, selling to organizations, not individuals.

The representative has several roles to fulfil. Being a two-way channel of communication between the company and its customers is one of the important ones. Identifying potential new customers is another.

Most important, however, is selling: persuading the customer to buy. This process will typically involve:

- projecting an honest, competent and confident image;
- identifying what satisfactions the customer is seeking and presenting the product in these terms;
- dealing with objections (the customer's arguments for not finalizing the sale, whether expressed or not);
- negotiating the price and other details;
- 'closing the sale'.

All this demands special skills, including communication (including using modern presentation techniques), negotiation and sales-specific skills such as being able to 'close' the sale. These are professional skills: they have to be learned, and they grow with experience.

At one time, the travelling representative was typically a 'loner', mobile, on the road for long periods and depending on his or her wits. This picture is a lot less true today. Most organizations think in terms of a sales team, in which a number of individuals, each with their own specialities, work together. They will try to build a relationship with a potential customer, win their confidence and then turn this into sales.

Busaco Materials was a newly formed UK subsidiary of a large Spanish supplier of building materials and equipment. It set up a sales team to try to carve itself out a market with UK building contractors. The team consisted of:

- Emma, a 'PA/secretary' whose job was to answer the phone, greet visitors and output correspondence, faxes and e-mails;
- Rahul, who processed orders and chased deliveries;
- Michael, the sales manager, in charge of the team as a whole;
- Isabella, accountant/estimator, responsible for preparing quotations for customers, and the only Spanish member of the team;

- Geoff, whose title was 'sales researcher': it was his job to find out when major new building projects were planned and to maintain a database on customers and competitors;
- Dorothy, sales executive; her job was to make initial contact with potential customers, to arrange sales presentations with them and to handle routine contacts thereafter; about half her time was spent out of the office.

A sales presentation would be attended by Michael, Isabella and Dorothy. Dorothy would prepare a slide show or computer-based presentation, plus other literature, and she and Michael would do most of the talking. If things went well, Michael would negotiate the details of the contract, with Isabella's help. Thereafter, Dorothy, Rahul and Geoff would be left to get on with things, under Michael's general supervision.

Activity 41

30 mins

Portfolio of evidence

S/NVQs A1.3, D1.1

This Activity may provide the basis of appropriate evidence for your S/NVQ portfolio. If you are intending to take this course of action, it might be better to write your answers on separate sheets of paper.

This Activity involves you in analysing the sales function in your own organization, or one that you know well. In particular, you will be looking at how the various people involved in selling work together as a team – and what their individual roles are.

You will need to talk to at least some of the people concerned. When you have done so, draw up a list of the team members and describe what role each plays.

Then make notes on how they work together to:

- decide how the 'sales pitch' will be put together;
- identify potential customers;
- make the initial contact;
- prepare for and handle sales meetings, presentations etc.;
- follow-up sales contacts.

Bear in mind that every organization will arrange its selling activities slightly differently. Some may well involve non-sales specialists like yourself in selling activities. You could also put forward your own proposals for improving the current set-up.

5.4 Back-up: caring for the customer

To do their job efficiently and effectively, the salesforce depends heavily on the support they get from their colleagues in the organization. Without this support, they may be unable to satisfy the customers' expectations and need – in both the short and the long term.

Activity 42 · 3 mins

What can a team supervisor in an office cleaning firm do to back up the efforts of the sales reps as they visit potential clients?

_____

_____

_____

_____

Back-up might take many forms.

- The reps may need information, as in the third example in Activity 17.
- They may need schedules or price lists posted out.
- They may want a supervisor to talk directly to the customer about some technical or procedural point.

At some stage, the customer may want to talk directly to the workteam, to try to judge how skilled and reliable they are. And the supervisor is highly likely to be involved in this.

But there is also a general point to make here: whenever you are in contact with people outside your organization, whether these are customers or not, you should always try to give the best possible impression. Another workbook in the series, _Caring for the Customer_, deals with customer-related aspects of marketing.

This returns us to the central issue of this workbook – the idea that in a modern, market-led organization, everyone on the payroll is part of the marketing mix, and that everyone can either help or hinder the marketing effort.

What do you do to 'sell' your organization? In the broadest possible sense we are all responsible for selling our organization, by:

- helping to give it a good public image by our own behaviour;
- taking every opportunity to help the marketing effort;
- being positive about the product;
- being supportive of the efforts of colleagues to develop the business.

In the world of the competitive market, it's the only way to survive.

Self-assessment 4

30 mins

Comment briefly on the following statements.

1 The art of pricing is to work out the cost of providing a product, from the initial idea through to distribution, and then add a margin for profit.

_____

_____

2 Distribution is a technical matter and has nothing to do with the marketing approach.

_____

_____

3 The chain of distribution can have many links or few.

_____

_____

4 Just-in-time delivery systems are highly inconvenient for the supplier and should be avoided.

_____

_____

5 Time is seldom a crucial part of the marketing mix because most customers allow plenty of lead time.

_____

_____

6 The old saying 'time is money' has little meaning today.

_____

_____

7 Distribution is not really an issue for service-type products such as security, office cleaning and insurance.

_____

_____

8 Customers should be realistic about delivery lead times and accept that producers can't keep disrupting production plans for their benefit.

_____

_____

9 Promotion is an activity which is best left to the specialists.

_____

_____

10 Everyone in an organization can help its marketing effort.

_____

_____

Answers to these questions can be found on page 97.

6 Summary

- It is no good having the right product if it isn't at the right price and isn't made available at the right place and time.

- Anything will sell if the price falls low enough. The art of pricing is to set a price which is:
  - high enough to make a profit;
  - low enough to create a demand.

- The simplest method of working out the price of a product is to add up all the costs involved and then add a margin for profit. This is the cost-plus method.

- The problem with this method is that it takes no account of what the market is prepared to pay.

- High-priced products can still sell, provided they are of high enough quality.

- The mechanism for getting manufactured products to the customer at the right place and time is the chain of production and distribution, which includes:
  - stock handling and storage;
  - physical distribution.

- Responsibility for ensuring that the product reaches the customer at the right place and time is shared by everybody working in: sales, administration, production and distribution.

- Managers, supervisors and team leaders have a particular responsibility to ensure that all their staff work towards this goal.

- Promotion and selling are the final important elements in the marketing mix. They can provide the competitive edge when a number of equally good products confront each other in the market place.

- Promotion is about using techniques to attract the customers' attention and arouse their interest.

- Selling is about personal skills to turn the customers' interest into action (i.e. a sale).

- In organizations where the selling is carried out by a specialized salesforce, other staff can still assist and provide back-up.

- In the final analysis, everyone in an organization has a role to play in helping the product to succeed.

Performance checks

1 Quick quiz

Jot down the answers to the following questions on *Marketing and Selling*.

Question 1   How would you define the term 'the market'?

_____

_____

Question 2   Why is it necessary for businesses to keep bringing new products onto the market?

_____

_____

Question 3   Define 'marketing'.

_____

_____

Question 4   What do we mean by the term 'the marketing approach'?

_____

_____

Question 5   What is the basic role of market research?

_____

_____

Question 6   What does it mean when we say an organization is 'product-led'?

_____

_____

Question 7   What do we mean by the term 'the marketing mix'?

_____

_____

Question 8   What factors and trends in the general environment are identified in a PESTLE analysis?

_____

_____

Question 9   What is the purpose of carrying out a SWOT analysis?

_____

_____

Question 10   Why do many organizations try to offer their markets a range of products at different levels of price?

_____

_____

Question 11   When you have worked out how much a product will cost to produce, what else do you have to do in order to set a selling price?

_____

_____

Question 12   What would the chain of production and distribution be for a TV assembled in the UK from a mixture of UK and foreign components?

_____

_____

Question 13   Why should non-commercial organizations consider adopting a marketing approach?

_____

_____

Question 14   What is the likely result of failing to get all the elements of the marketing mix right?

_____

_____

Question 15   What is the meaning of the letters AIDA?

_____

_____

_____

_____

Answers to these questions can be found on pages 99–100.

2 Workbook assessment

60 mins

Read the following case study and then deal with the questions that follow. Write your answers on a separate sheet of paper.

UK Flowlight is a regional distributor of solid fuels. It has small sales offices in about twenty towns, four depots and an administrative office in Corby. The total workforce is about eighty, of whom roughly two-thirds are part-timers.

The company was traditionally a coal merchant. Until the 1970s, its main products were home deliveries of coal for open fires and coke for boilers. In 1974 it still had 480 employees, but drastic market changes were in the offing. New laws on smoke emissions, industrial disputes in the coal industry and an increasing switch away from open fires towards gas central heating reduced the domestic solid fuels market by an average of 3% a year. The market is now only one-third of what it was in 1974, and the company has shrunk steadily.

86

Now its main products are various smokeless fuels; regular delivery runs cover the area from Derby in the north to Oxford in the south, and from Worcester and Shrewsbury in the west as far as King's Lynn in the east.

The company's owners feel that the domestic solid fuels market may now have stabilized, but there is a considerable amount of uncertainty about this. On the other hand, they think that there might be an opportunity to move into different markets that could be serviced from the same basic resources.

This is a change in the market with important implications for the people in the workteam – and for their supervisors. Think about the issues carefully, and then write down detailed notes which would enable you to answer the following questions.

1   What can UK Flowlight do to assess how the solid fuels market, and the company's position within it, are likely to change over the next ten years?

2   If the solid fuels market continues to shrink, and the firm can't find new markets, what does this imply for its future and that of its employees?

3   What assets does the firm have that might be put to other profitable uses?

4   Given these assets, and the expertise within the company, what other markets could it consider developing?

60 mins

3 Work-based assignment

Portfolio of evidence

S/NVQs A1.3, D1.1

The time guide for this assignment gives you an approximate idea of how long it is likely to take you to write up your findings. You will find you need to spend some additional time gathering information, talking to colleagues, and thinking about the assignment.

Your written response to this assignment may provide the basis of appropriate evidence for your S/NVQ portfolio.

Even if you don't deal with the customer face to face, you or other members of your team may have contact in writing or on the telephone. You almost certainly contribute to a product or a service which, ultimately, the customer uses.

Perhaps you feel that you don't have customers at all – especially if your job is providing information or services to other departments in the same organization. But, in that case, your customers are the colleagues that you serve: the people who use whatever you provide. Each customer contact is an opportunity to improve the relationship with that customer. Even a complaint, if dealt with correctly and promptly, can improve customer relations.

What you have to do

1 Make a list of all your customer contacts, both internal and external, with a note of the product or service (information, for example) that you supply to them.

2 Choose **five** customers from your list and write down one way in which you could improve the service to that customer, so that he or she gets:

- the right product;
- at the right price (if any);
- at the right place;
- at the right time;
- with the right promotion.

Reflect and review

1 Reflect and review

There are hundreds, if not thousands, of books, videos and training packages about marketing, but most of them deal with the technicalities of promotion, advertising, market research etc. Some, it is true, try to get to grips with the need to shape the product so as to meet the needs of the market. But few tackle the subject from the point of view of a non-specialist who wants to come to terms with 'the marketing approach'.

As you have seen throughout this workbook, marketing is not a cosmetic exercise – the 'icing on the cake'. It is about gearing the whole of the organization for market success, and everyone plays some kind of role in that.

Marketing is also about straight thinking. Ask yourself, 'What business are we in?' and the answer is only partly that you are in manufacturing, or retailing, or transport, or insurance, or local government or whatever. The most important answer is: 'We are first and foremost in the business of satsifying customers' needs.'

Your customers and their needs come first. They must determine what kind of product and service you offer and how you do so. If the product or service isn't right, then no amount of clever marketing will make it succeed.

The first workbook objective was as follows.

■ You will be better able to understand the meaning and importance of the market and the marketing approach.

The startling success of Japanese industry from the 1960s has been put down to many factors. First they were said to be 'good at copying other people's products', but then it became clear that 'they' were also extremely good at innovation. It used to be claimed that Japanese people had 'little fingers, so they were good at assembling tricky things'. That was nonsense too, as was talk about 'oriental self-discipline'. The Japanese have proved as good at banking as at electronics.

The reasons for Japan's success are complex, but two stand out, and they are both to do with attitude and ways of thinking. The first is that modern Japanese industry and commerce had to be re-built from scratch after World War II. The old markets, relationships and structures were destroyed, and a lot of old ideas, attitudes and ways of doing things were swept away with them.

The second factor was the new ideas that were brought in. The new Japanese industries had to face a world market almost from day one. They therefore **had** to adopt a 'marketing approach'. After the war, British car makers stolidly went on producing vehicles suitable for the winding roads and narrow streets of English counties, and they exported them on the assumption that they would do just as well in foreign markets. Their Japanese counterparts soon realized that foreign markets were different. They went out to acquire experience, and they designed and produced cars for success in those markets. This approach has been further refined in *kaizen*, or 'continuous improvement', which consciously sets out to improve process quality, and so maintain and improve competitiveness, year on year.

■ What would moving towards a marketing approach mean for you and your team? How can you explain this approach to them and motivate them to accept the changes in thinking and behaviour that may be needed?

_____

_____

_____

_____

The second objective was:

■ you will be better able to describe the main activities and tools of marketing.

At the centre of marketing activities is the marketing mix, which consists of the 'four Ps': product, price, place and promotion. Getting these right is essential if the organization is to be successful in meeting the needs of the customer. In a highly competitive world, any shortcoming in the marketing mix offers an opportunity for a competitor to gain an advantage. Everyone on the payroll contributes to the marketing mix in some way, once it has been established what the mix should be.

A number of tools can be used in the effort to identify the right marketing mix. One of these is PESTLE analysis, which helps the manager to think about a wide range of factors in the external environment – political, economic, social, technological, legal and environmental – that may have an effect on the organization in the future. Such factors may mean making changes in the marketing mix if the organization is to remain successful. The nature of these changes begins to become apparent when a SWOT analysis is carried out. This not only identifies the opportunities and threats presented by the environment, but also the strengths and weaknesses of the organization itself – and hence its ability, or inability, to respond to what is happening in the environment. A SWOT analysis is an essential part of the marketing plan, in which objectives are drawn up that will result in changes to the marketing mix in the future.

■ What are the main features of your organization's marketing mix at present? What ideas do you have about how the mix might be changed in the future?

_____
_____
_____
_____
_____
_____

Having worked through the four sessions of this workbook, you may already be applying the ideas we have discussed both personally and with your workteam. Once you start thinking in terms of the marketing approach, you will find many opportunities to make a positive contribution to the organization's success in the market.

The final workbook objective sums up the overall theme.

■ You will be better able to adopt the marketing approach and apply it to your everyday activities.

■ What are you now doing that is different from before?

_____
_____
_____
_____

■ What more will you do in the future to apply the marketing approach?

_____
_____
_____
_____

2 Action plan

Use this plan to further develop for yourself a course of action you want to take. Make a note in the left-hand column of the issues or problems you want to tackle, and then decide what you intend to do, and make a note in column 2.

The resources you need might include time, materials, information or money. You may need to negotiate for some of them, but they could be something easily acquired, like half an hour of somebody's time, or a chapter of a book. Put whatever you need in column 3. No plan means anything without a timescale, so put a realistic target completion date in column 4.

Finally, describe the outcome you want to achieve as a result of this plan, whether it is for your own benefit or advancement, or a more efficient way of doing things.

Desired outcomes				
1 Issues	2 Action		3 Resources	4 Target completion
Actual outcomes				

3 Extensions

Extension 1

Book   *Do Your Own Market Research*
Authors   P.N. Hague and P. Jackson
Edition   3rd, 1998
Publisher   Kogan Page
ISBN   0749426527

There are, of course, practical limits on what an individual can do in terms of market research, and books of this type are mainly intended for people running their own small businesses. Even so, there are plenty of practical suggestions here that someone working for a larger company could adopt to find out more about their customers.

Extension 2

Book   *Marketing Made Simple*
Authors   G. Lancaster and P. Reynolds
Edition   2002
Publisher   Made Simple Books
ISBN   075064771X

Literally thousands of books about marketing have been written over the years, and hundreds are in print today. Some are specialized – dealing with marketing for small businesses, marketing services, international marketing etc. This one is a good general approach with plenty of useful examples.

Extension 3

Book   *Marketing Tool Kit*
Author   N. Robinson
Edition   2nd, 2002
Publisher   Management Books 2000
ISBN   1852520388

Advertising and many other promotional techniques are a specialist area. This book provides an overview of the various techniques for the non-specialist reader.

Extension 4

Book   *The New Strategic Selling*
Authors   Stephen E. Heiman, Diane Sanchez and Tad Tuleja
Edition   1988
Publisher   Kogan Page

This book has become a business classic. It is based on the sales process used by companies such as Coca-Cola and IBM – the Miller Heiman sales training programme. Unlike many books on selling, it focuses on clear, practical steps you can use in selling and managing the sales process.

I recommend that you take up as many of the extensions as you can. They will further increase your understanding and interest, and the extra time and effort will prove very worthwhile.

These Extensions can be taken up via your ILM Centre. They will either have them or will arrange that you have access to them. However, it may be more convenient to check out the materials with your personnel or training people at work – they may well give you access. There are other good reasons for approaching your own people; for example, they will become aware of your interest and you can involve them in your development.

4 Answers to self-assessment questions

Self-assessment 1 on page 16

1 These statements should read as follows:

   a The market forces traders to face **competition** and presents customers with **choice**.
   b The market is the net result of millions of individual **purchasing decisions**.
   c The term **product** refers to whatever an organization offers to the market.
   d Even the most successful product has a limited **life-cycle** [or **life-time**].
   e Market research is about gaining greater **knowledge** and **understanding** of the market.

2 The statement that best describes the marketing approach is c. **It is about identifying and satisfying customer needs**.

3 A **market-led** organization is one that studies its market before getting a product produced. A **product-led** organization is one that produces what it considers to be a superb product first and then sets about discovering whether it is what customers want.

Reflect and review

Self-assessment 2 on page 34

1   The marketing mix is the sum total of all the elements that make up the 'offer' that an organization makes to its market.

2   The four main elements of the marketing mix are:

■ product;
■ price;
■ place;
■ promotion.

3   The three 'behind-the-scenes factors' that most affect long-term customer loyalty are:

■ the speed with which problems and complaints are tackled;
■ the attitude of the staff;
■ the general efficiency of the organization.

Self-assessment 3 on pages 52–3

1   Signs that a product is meeting the needs of the market are:

■ sales or take-up are on or above **target**;
■ the number of approving letters or phone calls from **customers** goes up;
■ there is a low number of **complaints**.

2   The six different types of factors or trends that a PESTLE analysis is concerned with are:
■ Political
■ Economic
■ Social
■ Technological
■ Legal
■ Environmental

3   A segment of the market is a distinct slice of the market that demands particular things from a product range. These things are different from those demanded by other segments.

4   In a SWOT analysis, the letters S, W, O and T stand for the following.

■ Strengths
■ Weaknesses
■ Opportunities
■ Threats

5   A SWOT analysis is an important part of a marketing plan because it indicates ways in which an organization can – or cannot – move forward in the future and so helps a manager to decide on possible marketing objectives.

Self-assessment 4 on page 79–80

1   The art of pricing is more than working out the cost of producing a product and then adding a margin for profit – the 'cost-plus' method. The art of pricing is, in fact, to set a price that is high enough to make a profit and low enough to create a demand.

2   This statement is quite misleading. The ability to provide the product at the right place and time is a crucial part of the marketing mix.

3   The number of links in the chain can vary greatly. When a smallholder sells his or her own cheese and honey direct to consumers, no other links are needed. On the other hand, where a product is assembled in the Far East, sold wholesale to a trader in Italy and then distributed in batches to a variety of other traders throughout the EU, before filtering down to local retailers in the UK, the links may be many.

4   It is unfortunate if meeting the needs of the customer seems inconvenient, because a competitor will be prepared to do what the customer wants and thus gain the customer.

5   Time is very important – suppliers must be able to meet their agreed dates and times and, all other things being equal, the supplier who can provide the product soonest often wins the order.

6   The concept that 'time is money' is even more important than it has ever been, because of the much greater scale, speed and value of all commercial transactions.

7   Service organizations don't distribute in the way that manufacturers of physical products do; all the same, they have to make sure that their product is able to reach their customers (or perhaps vice versa). A college, for example, sells courses and skills. It may need to reach out beyond its local catchment by setting up 'satellite units' or offering courses by distance learning.

8   Customers are often prepared to be flexible when dealing with an established supplier, but no supplier should bank on this. In principle, the customer's needs should override those of the supplier.

9   While this is true, it doesn't mean that managers, supervisors and team leaders elsewhere in the organization can afford to ignore it.

10 I hope you agree with this statement: it is the main message of this workbook!

5 Answers to Activities

**Activity 37
on page 70**

Anything which relates to Christmas, from puddings to wrapping paper, is subject to seasonal demand. Easter eggs and fireworks are examples of the same kind of thing. But jewellery is also very seasonal, for the same reasons as toys. And there are also definite seasonal peaks in demand for:

- patio sets;
- lawnmowers;
- seeds and fertilizer;
- caravans;
- camping equipment;
- sunglasses;
- suntan lotion;
- swimwear;
- outdoor coats;
- gloves;
- bicycles;
- antifreeze;
- coal.

**Activity 40
on page 75**

- Examples of type 1 include many furniture stores, some shoe shops, and many hi-fi specialists.
- Examples of type 2 include department stores and firms such as Woolworths or Boots.
- Examples of type 3 include self-service stores, especially supermarkets.

6 Answers to the quick quiz

Answer 1   The market is the net result of the coming together of limitless numbers of buyers and sellers, and hence of millions of individual purchasing decisions.

Answer 2   Businesses need to keep bringing new products onto the market because all products have a limited life-cycle, and new products are needed to replace them.

Answer 3   Marketing is the process of identifying and satisfying the needs of the customer.

Answer 4   The marketing approach means gearing every aspect of an organization's activity towards satisfying the needs of the customer.

Answer 5   Market research is about gaining greater knowledge and understanding of the market. Market researchers try to find out about the present state of the market – who is selling what to whom, and for how much – and how this is likely to change in the future.

Answer 6   A product-led organization is one that develops products first and looks for markets afterwards.

Answer 7   The marketing mix is the sum total of all the things that an organization does that have some impact on customers' attitudes to its products – the total 'offer' that the organization makes to its market.

Answer 8   The factors and trends identified in a PESTLE analysis are political, economic, social, technological, legal and environmental.

Answer 9   The purpose of carrying out a SWOT analysis is to identify the strengths and weaknesses of an organization, and the opportunities and threats presented by the general environment. This makes it an important tool in the process of planning the way forward and producing marketing objectives.

Answer 10   Many organizations try to offer a range of products because this enables them to reach a larger total market while using the same basic skills and resources.

Answer 11   Cost price is the basis of a selling price, but this can only be set after considering what competitors are offering, and what the market is prepared to pay.

Answer 12   The chain of production here will be a complicated one:

- raw material extracting and processing;
- manufacture and importation of components from several different locations;
- distribution, possibly through a number of different channels;
- retailing to the customer.

Answer 13   Non-commercial organizations should consider adopting a marketing approach because they, too, are providing products or services to their customers. They are increasingly subject to commercial pressures, and their customers are increasingly demanding to be treated as such.

Answer 14   If anything in the marketing mix isn't right, this will give competitors an advantage.

Answer 15   AIDA stands for Attention, Interest, Desire, Action – the process that advertisers and other communicators use to get results.

7 Certificate

Completion of this certificate by an authorized person shows that you have worked through all the parts of this workbook and satisfactorily completed the assessments. The certificate provides a record of what you have done that may be used for exemptions or as evidence of prior learning against other nationally certificated qualifications.

Pergamon Open Learning and ILM are always keen to refine and improve their products. One of the key sources of information to help this process are people who have just used the product. If you have any information or views, good or bad, please pass these on.

INSTITUTE OF LEADERSHIP & MANAGEMENT

SUPERSERIES

Marketing and Selling

....

has satisfactorily completed this workbook

Name of signatory   ....

Position   ....

Signature   ....

Date   ....

Official stamp

Fourth Edition

INSTITUTE OF LEADERSHIP & MANAGEMENT
SUPER SERIES
FOURTH EDITION

Achieving Quality	0 7506 5874 6
Appraising Performance	0 7506 5838 X
Becoming More Effective	0 7506 5887 8
Budgeting for Better Performance	0 7506 5880 0
Caring for the Customer	0 7506 5840 1
Collecting Information	0 7506 5888 6
Commitment to Equality	0 7506 5893 2
Controlling Costs	0 7506 5842 8
Controlling Physical Resources	0 7506 5886 X
Delegating Effectively	0 7506 5816 9
Delivering Training	0 7506 5870 3
Effective Meetings at Work	0 7506 5882 7
Improving Efficiency	0 7506 5871 1
Information in Management	0 7506 5890 8
Leading Your Team	0 7506 5839 8
Making a Financial Case	0 7506 5892 4
Making Communication Work	0 7506 5875 4
Managing Change	0 7506 5879 7
Managing Lawfully – Health, Safety and Environment	0 7506 5841 X
Managing Lawfully – People and Employment	0 7506 5853 3
Managing Relationships at Work	0 7506 5891 6
Managing Time	0 7506 5877 0
Managing Tough Times	0 7506 5817 7
Marketing and Selling	0 7506 5837 1
Motivating People	0 7506 5836 3
Networking and Sharing Information	0 7506 5885 1
Organizational Culture and Context	0 7506 5884 3
Organizational Environment	0 7506 5889 4
Planning and Controlling Work	0 7506 5813 4
Planning Training and Development	0 7506 5860 6
Preventing Accidents	0 7506 5835 5
Project and Report Writing	0 7506 5876 2
Securing the Right People	0 7506 5822 3
Solving Problems	0 7506 5818 5
Storing and Retrieving Information	0 7506 5894 0
Understanding Change	0 7506 5878 9
Understanding Finance	0 7506 5815 0
Understanding Quality	0 7506 5881 9
Working In Teams	0 7506 5814 2
Writing Effectively	0 7506 5883 5

To order – phone us direct for prices and availability details
(please quote ISBNs when ordering) on 01865 888190